AF469849

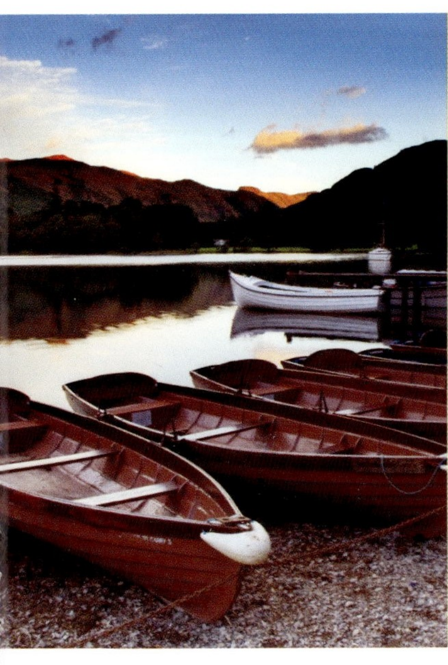

THE SPIRIT OF
CUMBRIA

JASON FRIEND

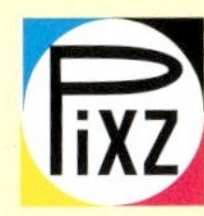

First published in Great Britain in 2009

Copyright text and photographs © 2009 Jason Friend/Jason Friend Photography Ltd
All images in this book can be licensed via www.jasonfriendimages.co.uk

Title page: Rowing boats on the shore of Ullswater, the second longest lake to be found in Cumbria.

All rights reserved. No part of this publication may be reproduced,
stored in a retrieval system, or transmitted in any form or by any
means without the prior permission of the copyright holder.

British Library Cataloguing-in-Publication Data
A CIP record for this title is available from the British Library

ISBN 978 1 906887 00 1

PiXZ Books
Halsgrove House, Ryelands Industrial Estate, Bagley Road,
Wellington, Somerset TA21 9PZ
Tel: 01823 653777
Fax: 01823 216796
email: sales@halsgrove.com

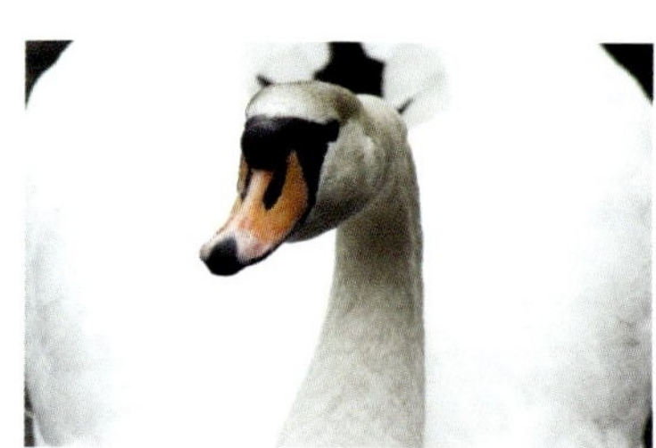

An imprint of Halstar Ltd, part of the Halsgrove group of companies
Information on all Halsgrove ttles is available at: www.halsgrove.com

Printed and bound by D'Auria Industrie Grafiche, Italy

Introduction

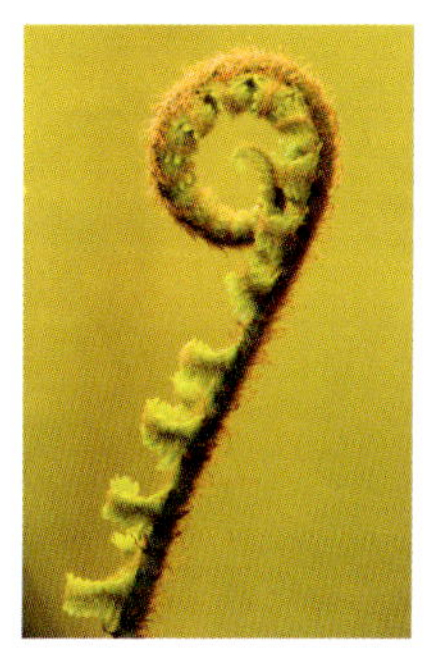

In excess of 12 million people visit the county of Cumbria every year, some opting to relax within the quintessential English villages to be found here, whilst others choose to exchange the familiarity of urban life for some time exploring the numerous fells and lakes. The region is home to the deepest and largest lakes as well as the highest peaks to be found in the country. These all fall within the boundaries of perhaps the most famous of all of the English National Parks – The Lake District.

However, there is much more than the Lake District National Park to explore here. The Howgills and the northern Pennines afford commanding views across the county to the visitor originating from the east, whilst the distant form of the fells and peaks, for any visitor heading from the north or south, offers a more subtle introduction to the region. The Irish Sea borders the west of the county with the nearest neighbours being the Isle of Man and Scotland, whose uplands can be viewed rising from across the peaceful Solway Firth.

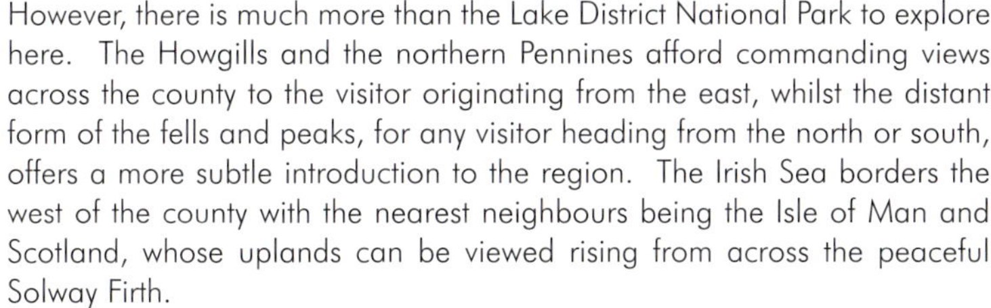

Weather has a huge impact on the region that is understandable if you consider that it is in fact the wettest place to be found in England, although if you visit on a hot summer's day you would be forgiven for not believing the statistics. Four seasons in one day is not an uncommon experience to encounter here, but perhaps this is what helps to create the true essence of the county, alongside the picturesque landscape and the events of history. Given this combination, maybe we could consider this to be the true spirit of Cumbria.

Acknowledgments

I cannot take all of the credit for the production of this book so I would like to acknowledge the following people who have helped out behind the scenes in one form or another.

Thank you to everyone who has joined me on my numerous outings to Cumbria over the past years including Mark Whitehouse, Wayne Hackeson and Lynette Friend. I am extremely grateful to Dave Clayton of A1scan.co.uk for the scanning of a selection of the panoramic images and Steven Pugsley and the rest of the team at Halsgrove for making this book a reality.

The support of family and friends is an important ingredient when working on a book of any size so I would like to wholeheartedly thank all of you including John Friend, Penny and Roy Whitehouse, Valerie Hodgkins, Steven Turner, Steve Hawthorne and Jason Haynes.

An extra special thank you must go to Lynette for her support and encouragement over the years and for giving me the honour of become my wife at our wedding in the heart of the Lake District during the undertaking of this project.

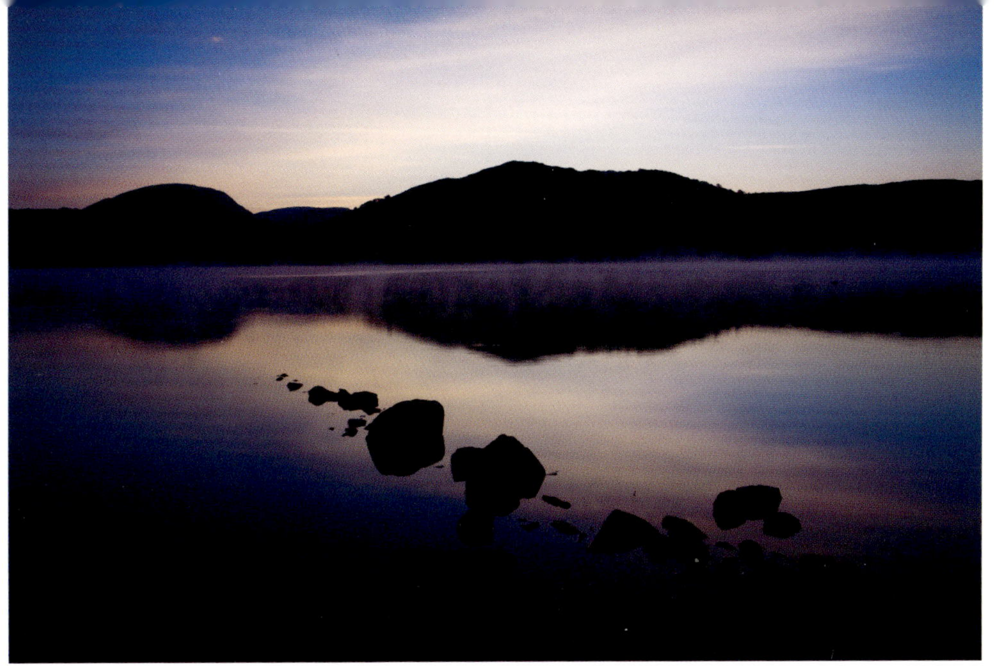

Dawn at Low Wray, looking across the still waters of Windermere, the largest lake to be found in England. Early morning mist gently rises from the glass-like surface on a clear spring morning.

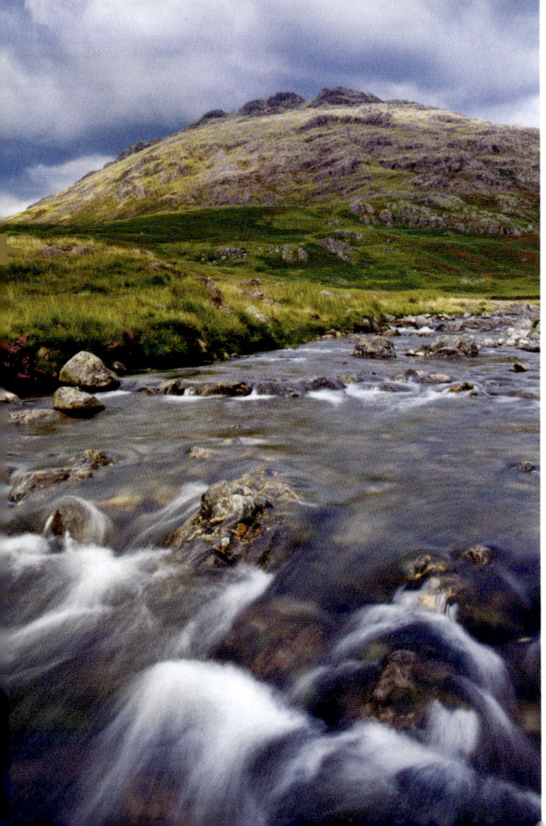

River Duddon and storm clouds above
the Little Stand and Ulpha Fell.

Opposite page:
Soft evening light bathes a solitary cottage
situated within the barren landscape of the
Pennines, near the isolated town of Alston.

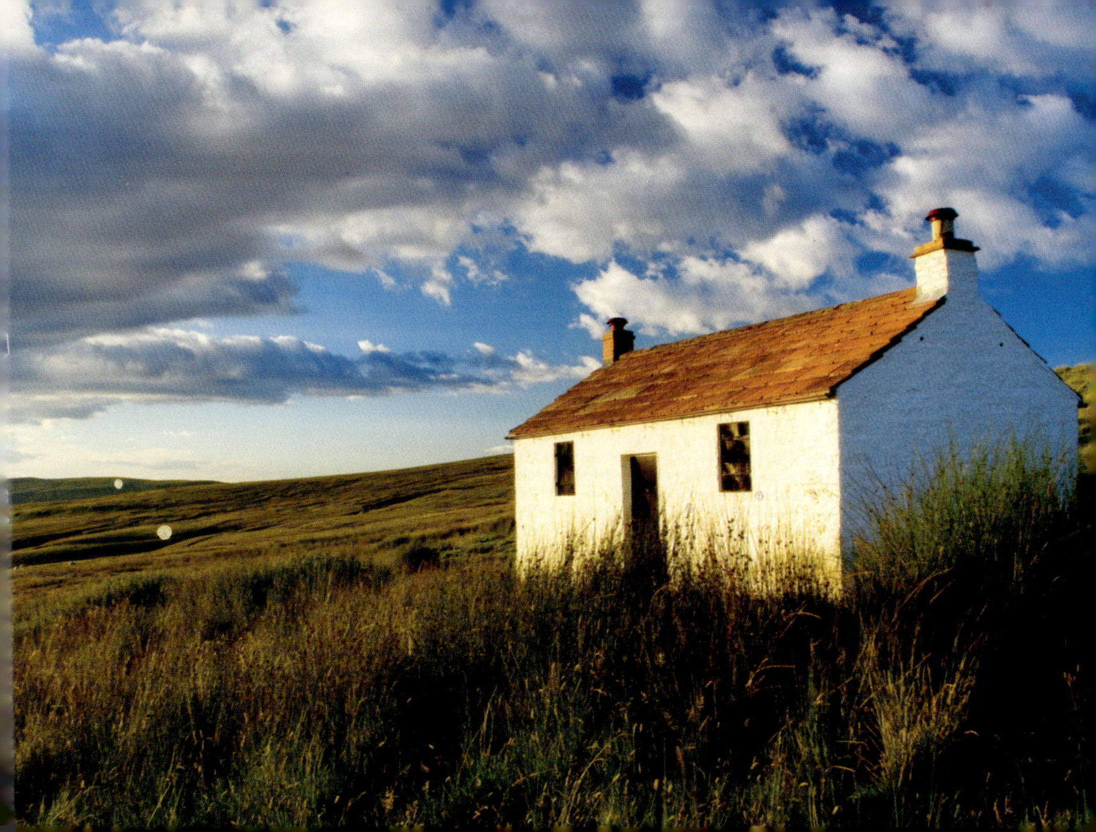

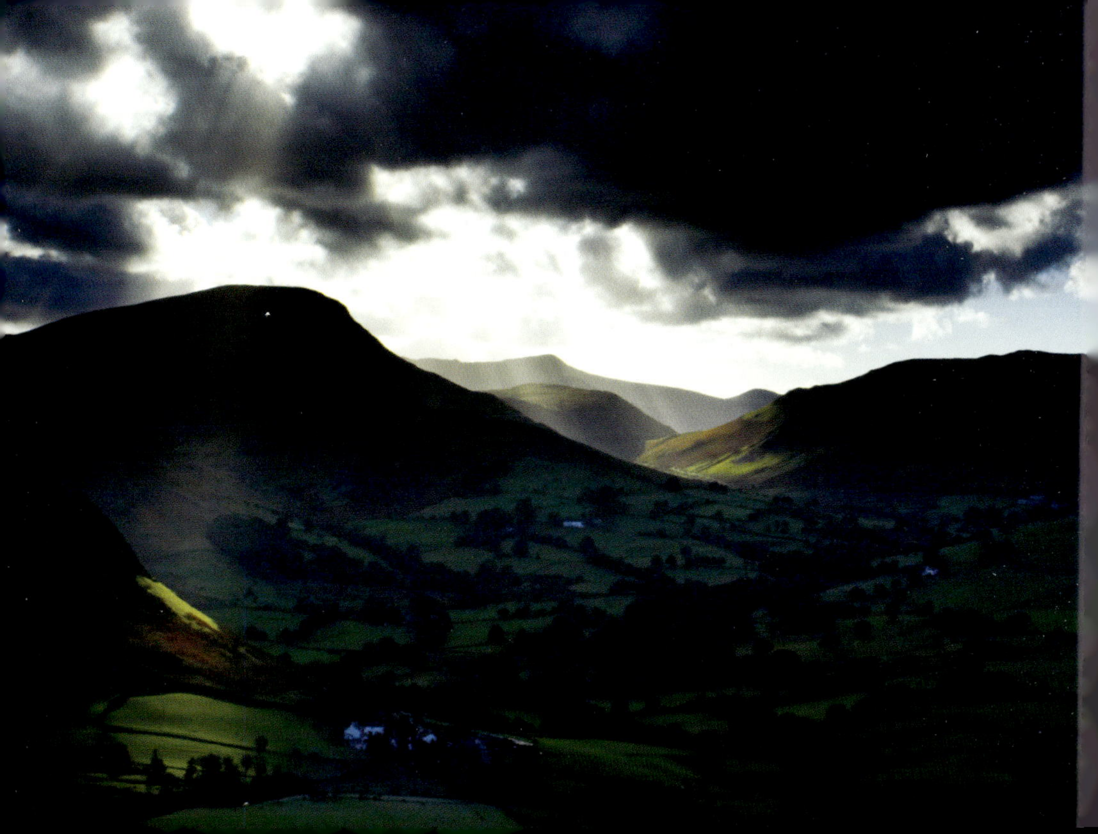

Looking along the route of the River Esk from the Hardknott Castle Roman Fort, as storm clouds gather above the country's highest peak, Scafell Pike at 3205ft.

Opposite page:
Brief shafts of light break through storm clouds illuminating the features of the Newlands Valley.

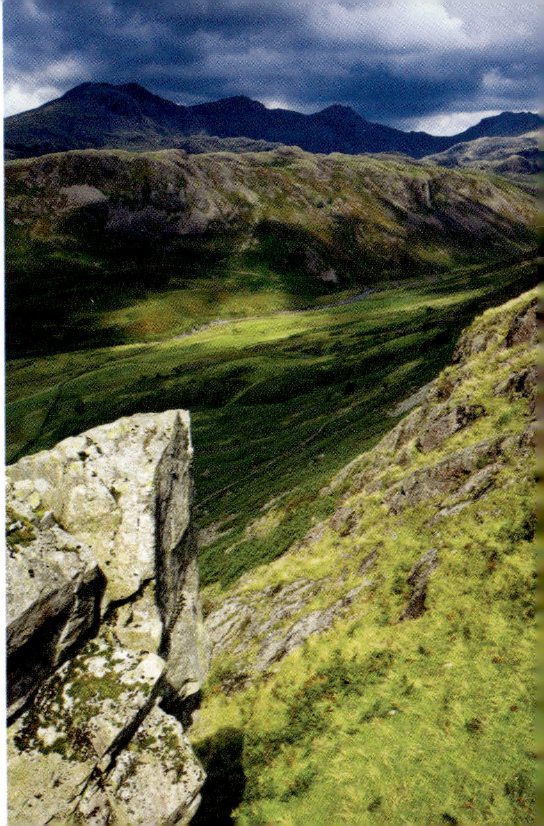

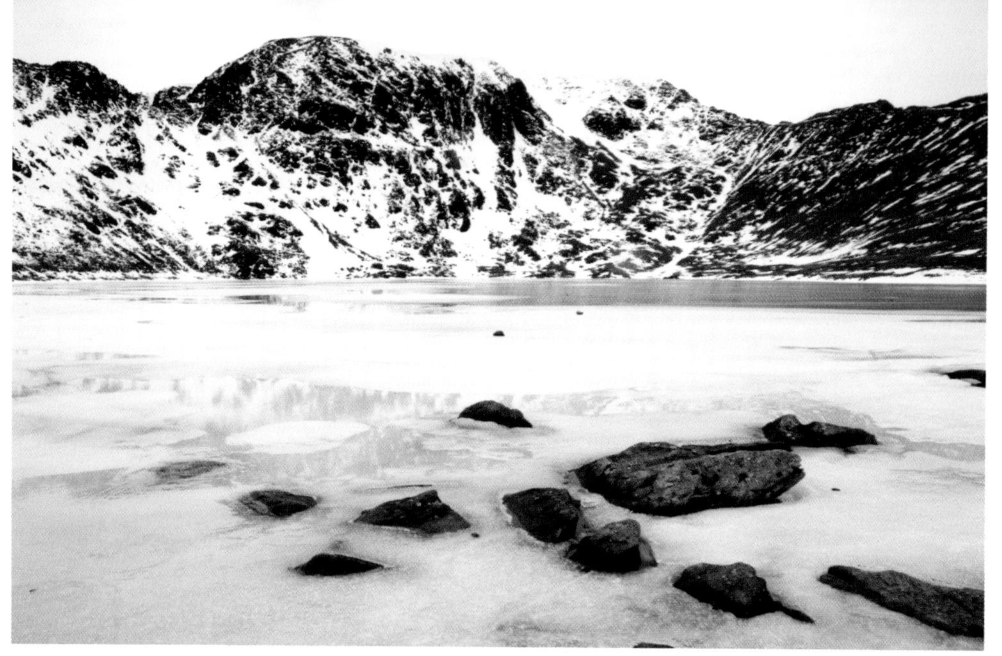

The ice-covered expanse of Red Tarn, beneath the snow-capped peaks of Helvellyn.

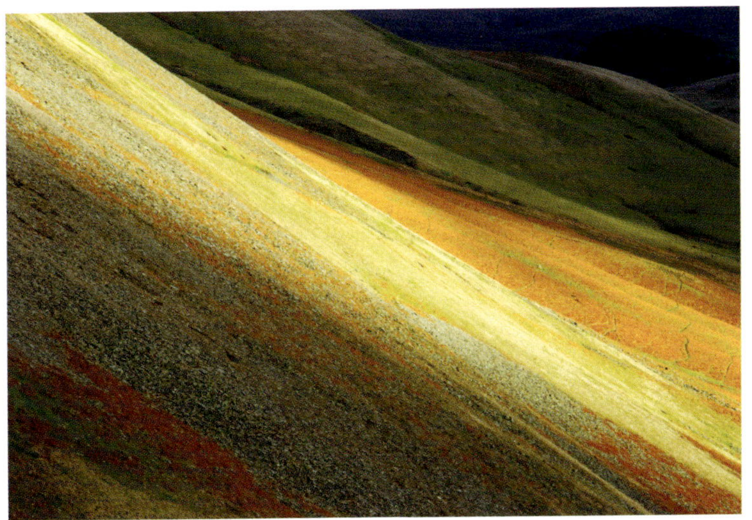

A shaft of light illuminates the hills of the Yorkshire Dales National Park,
located to the north east of the town of Sedbergh. Despite the name of the park,
this section is actually within the boundaries of Cumbria.

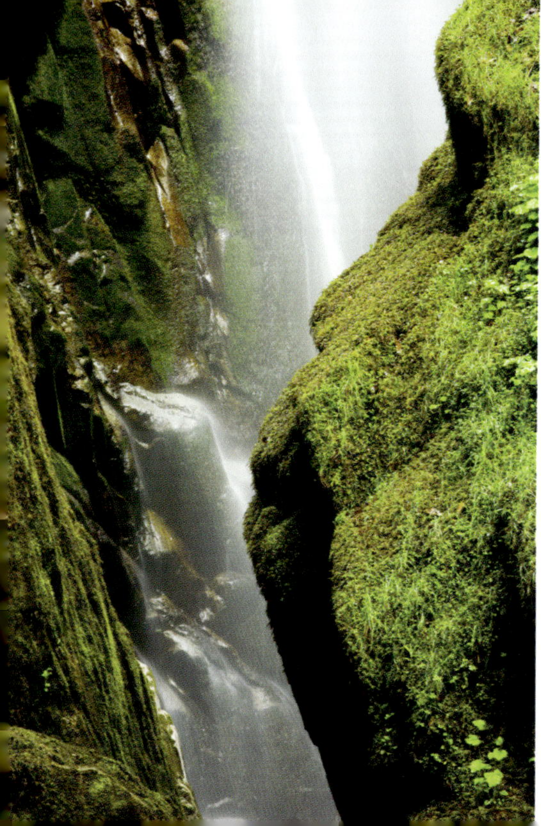

Aira Force is a powerful body of water near the shores of Ullswater. A circular walk encompasses the falls, with a picturesque stone bridge providing the means to cross the 70ft dramatic drop of water.

Opposite page:
A hiker descending from Angle Tarn towards Dungeon Ghyll in the Great Langdale Valley.

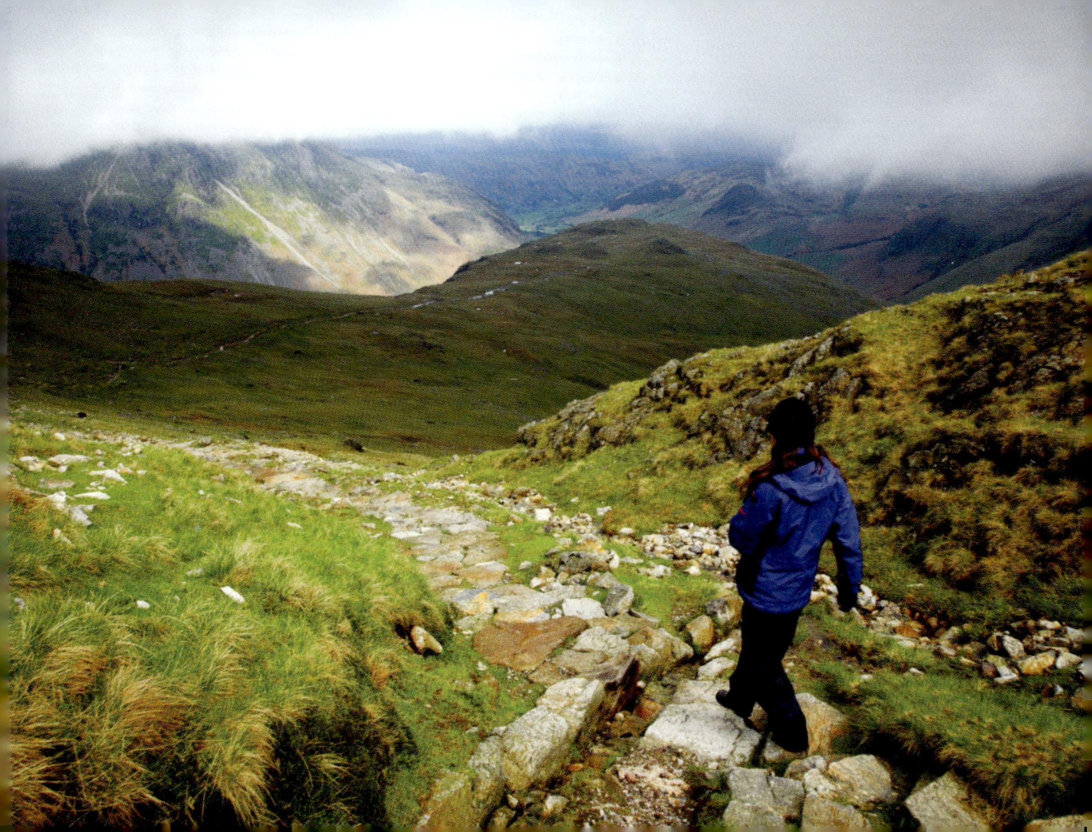

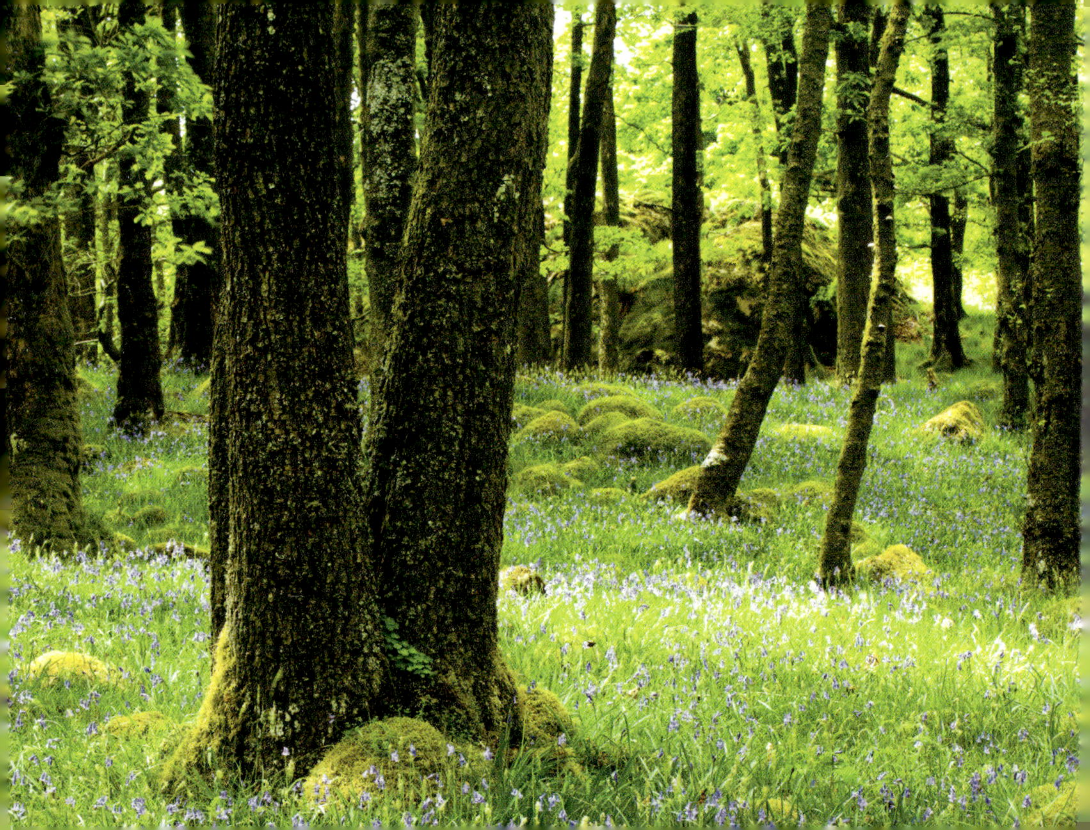

A forest-covered hill reflected in Yew Tree
Tarn is a scene typical of the Lake District.

Opposite page:
A blanket of flowering Bluebells
adds a splash of spring colour to
Dunnerdale Forest.

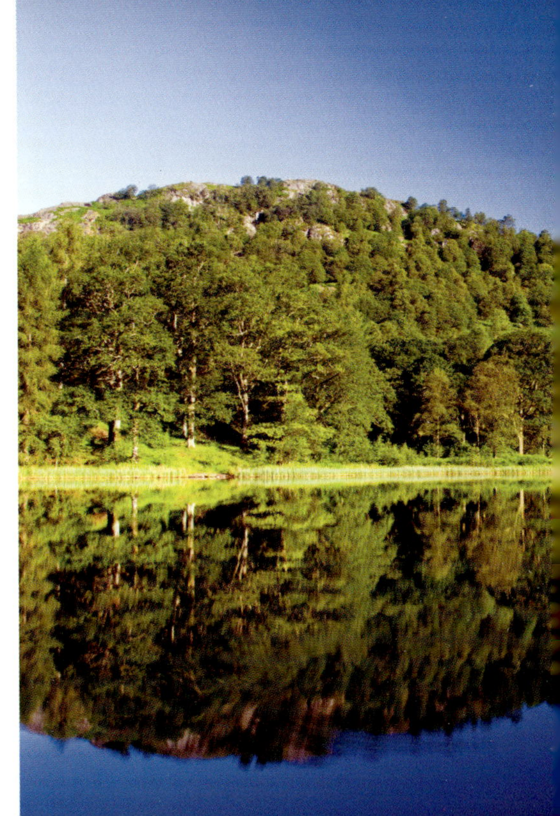

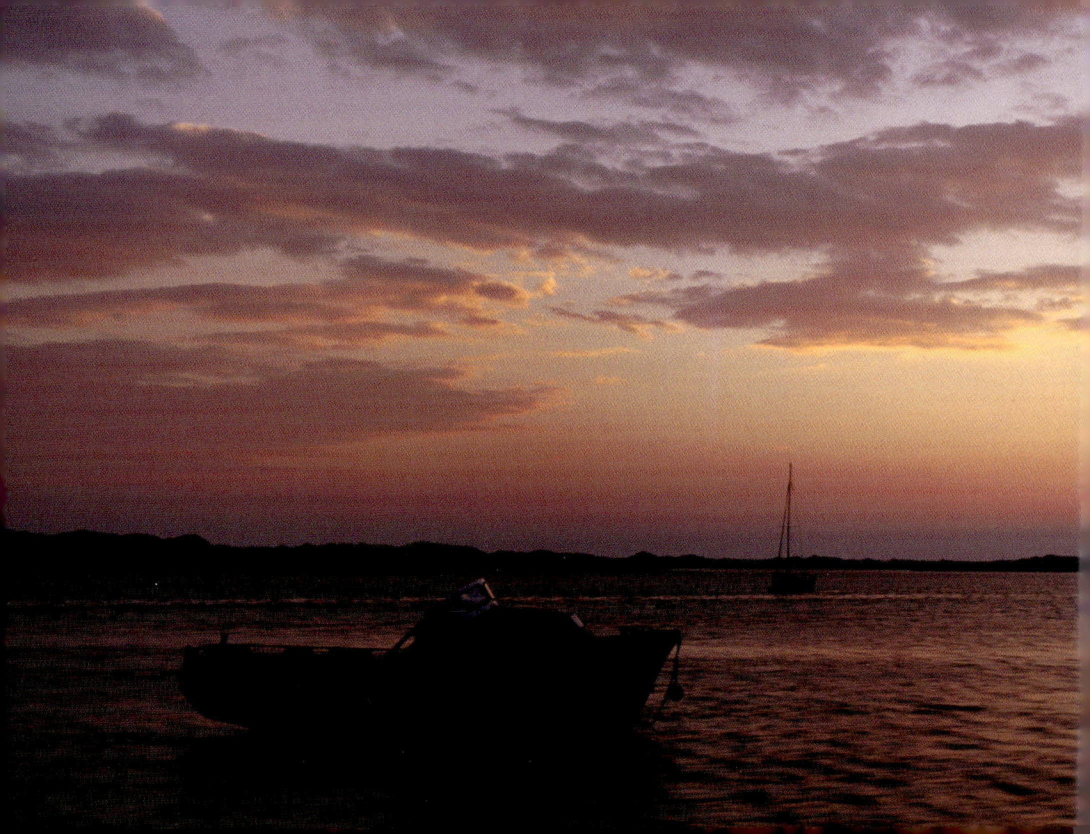

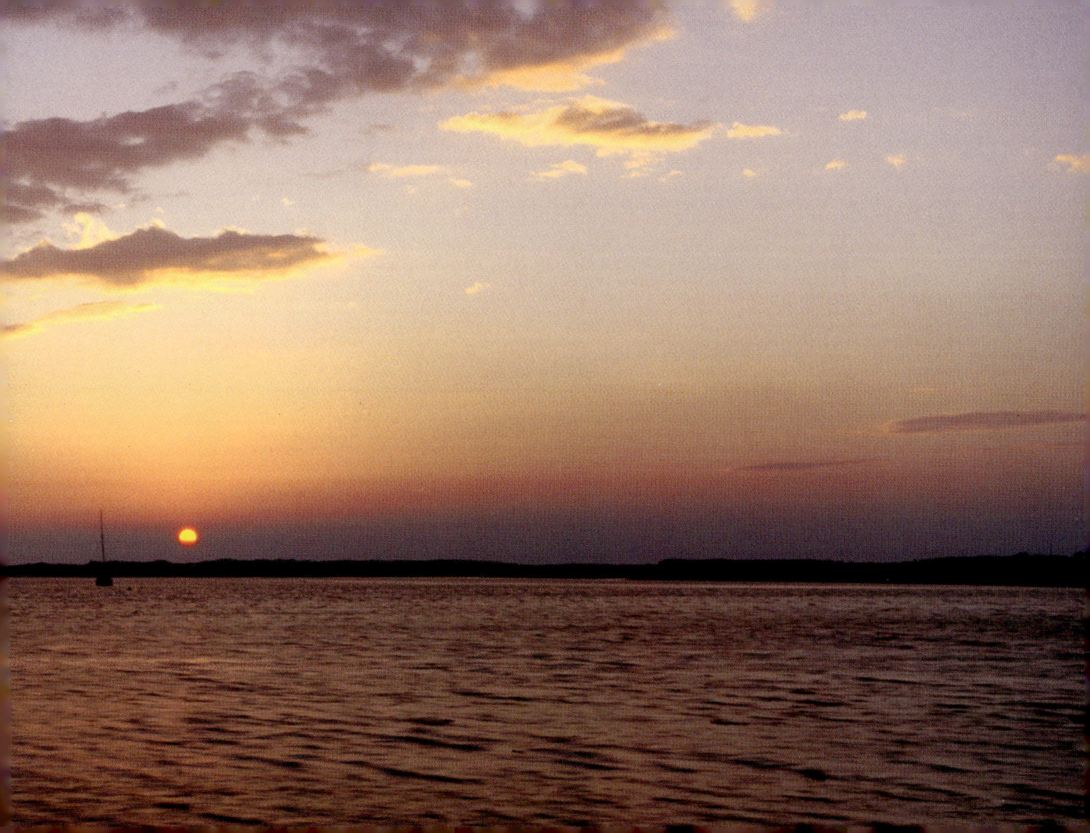

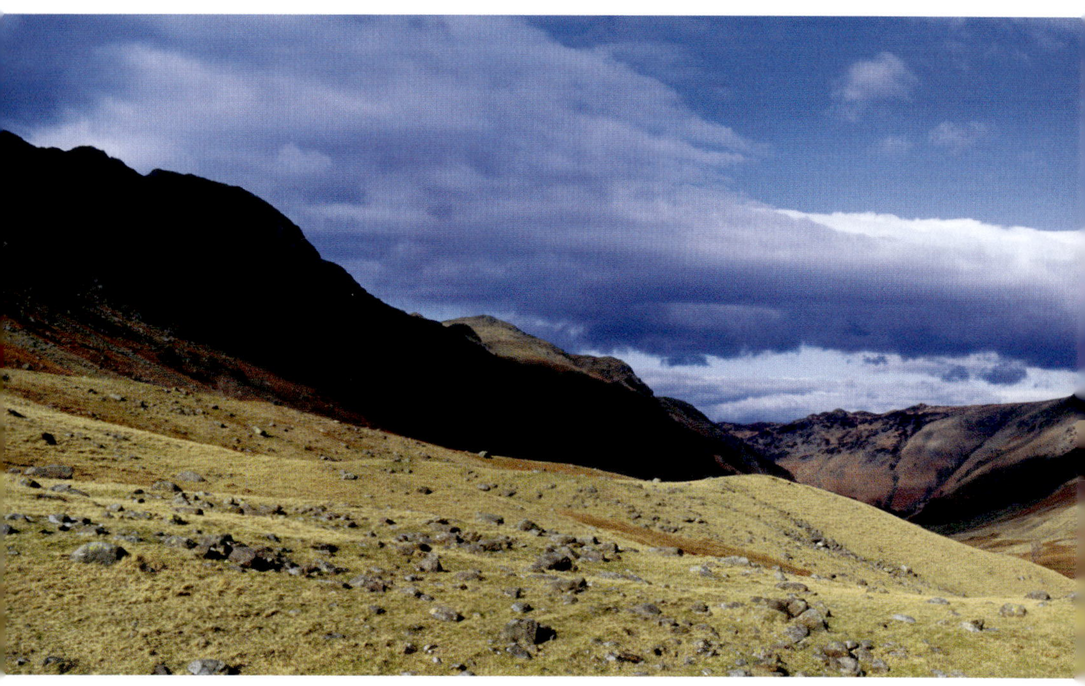

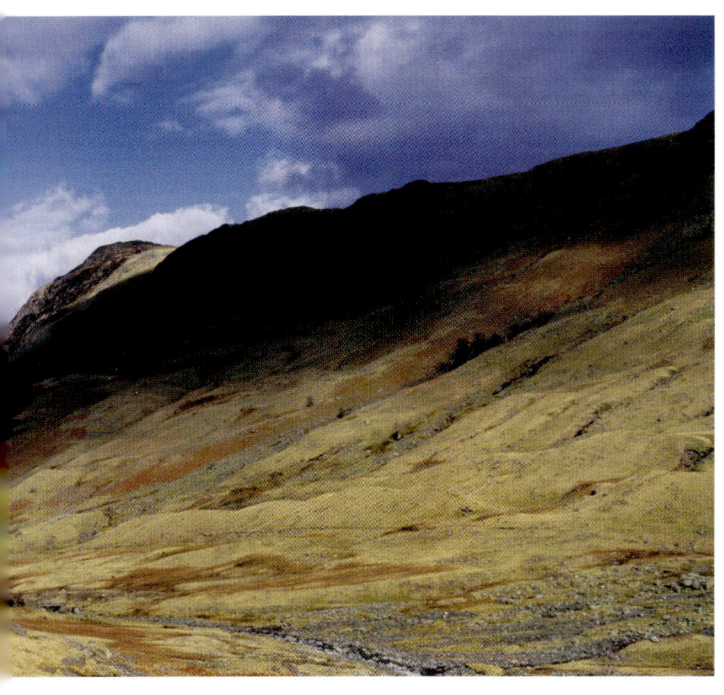

Brief shafts of sun
illuminate the
surrounding peaks of
the Langstrath Valley.

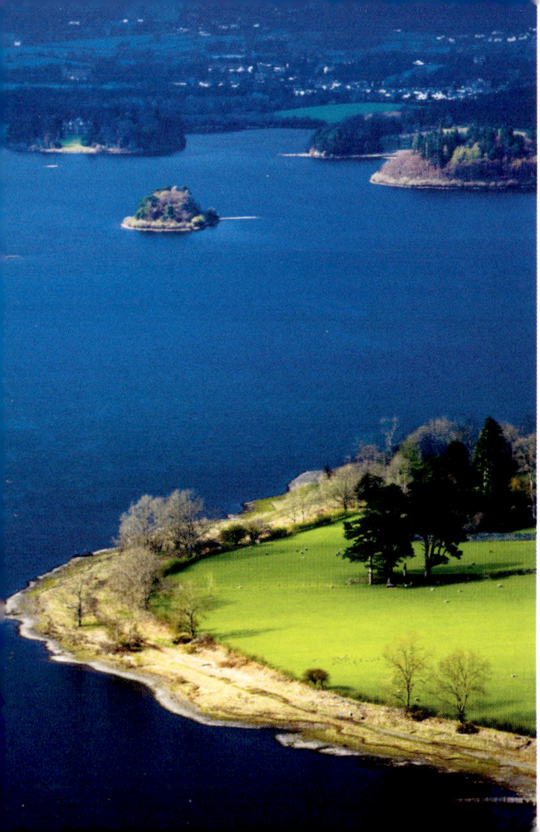

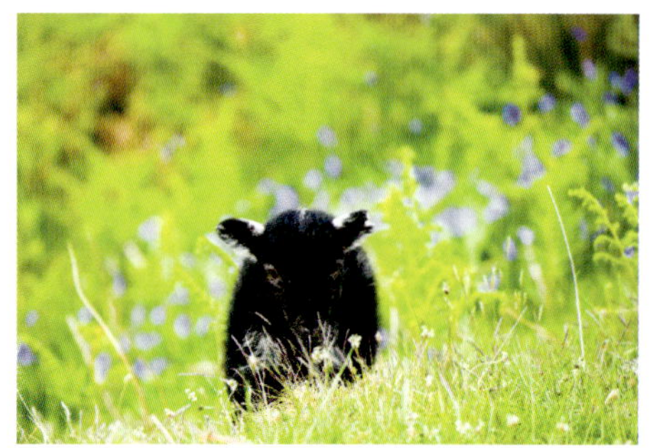

Black lamb hiding in wild flowers on a fell near Dunnerdale Forest.

Left:
Derwentwater, with Derwent Island and Keswick in the distance, viewed from Surprise View on Gowder Crag.

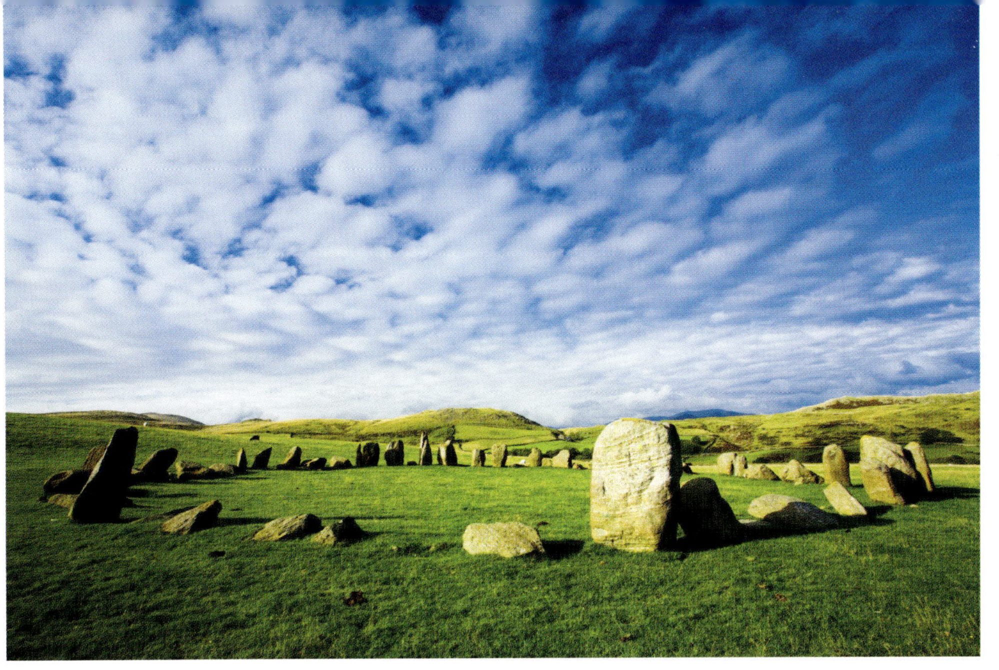

The name of the Sunkenkirk stone circle, also known as Swinside, is derived from the ancient belief that the circle of stones is what remains of an ancient church (kirk) sunk into the ground by a strike from the Devil.

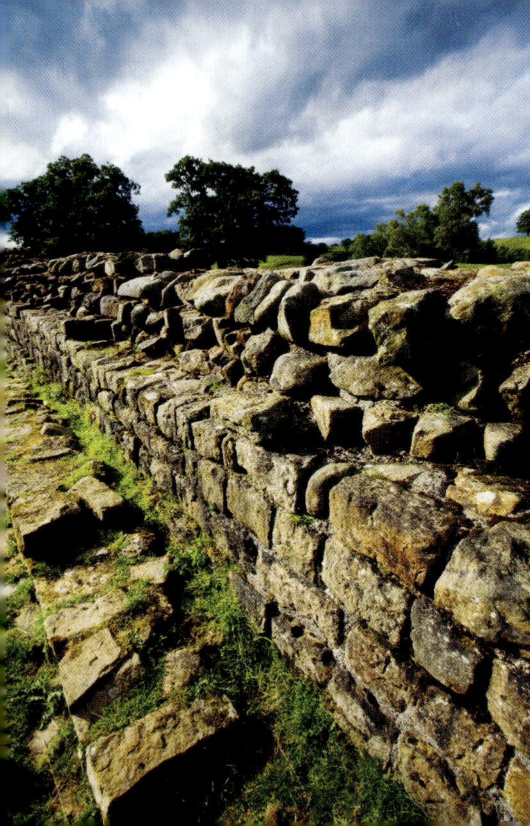

The Hadrian's Wall long distance track running alongside Hadrian's Wall near Gilsland, forming part of the Hadrian's Wall UNESCO World Heritage Site.

Opposite page:
A display of bluebells within Great Wood in Borrowdale.

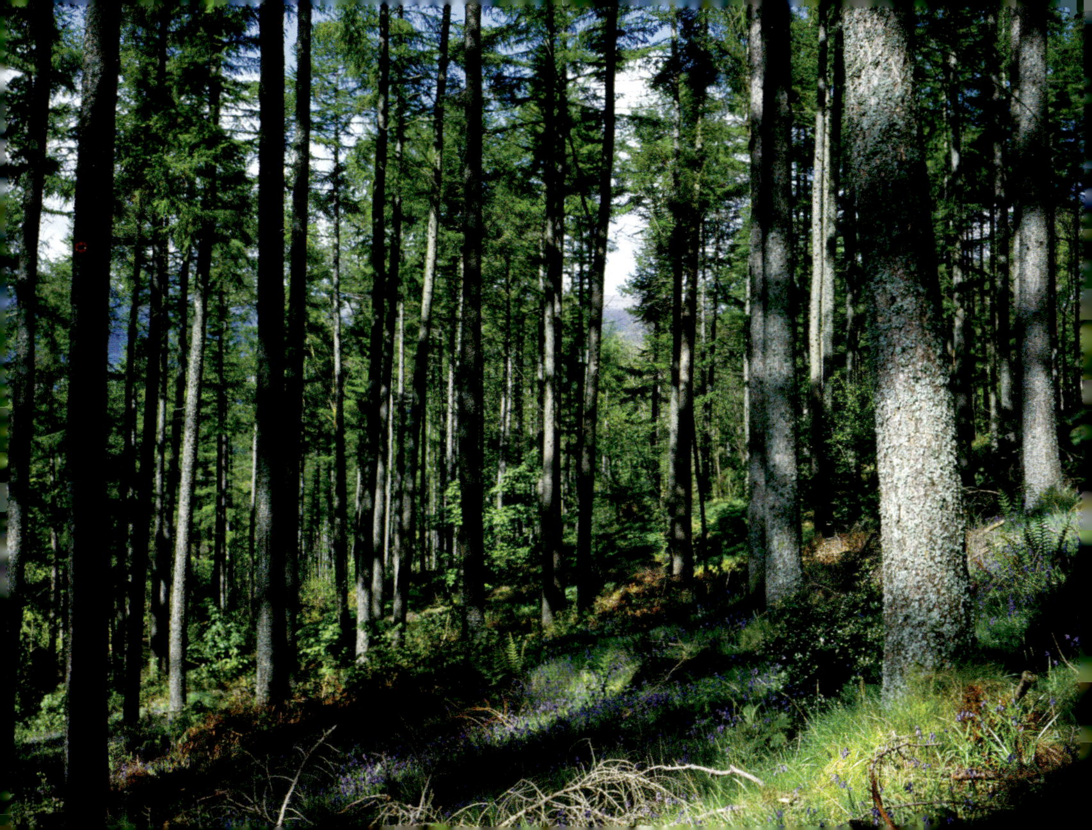

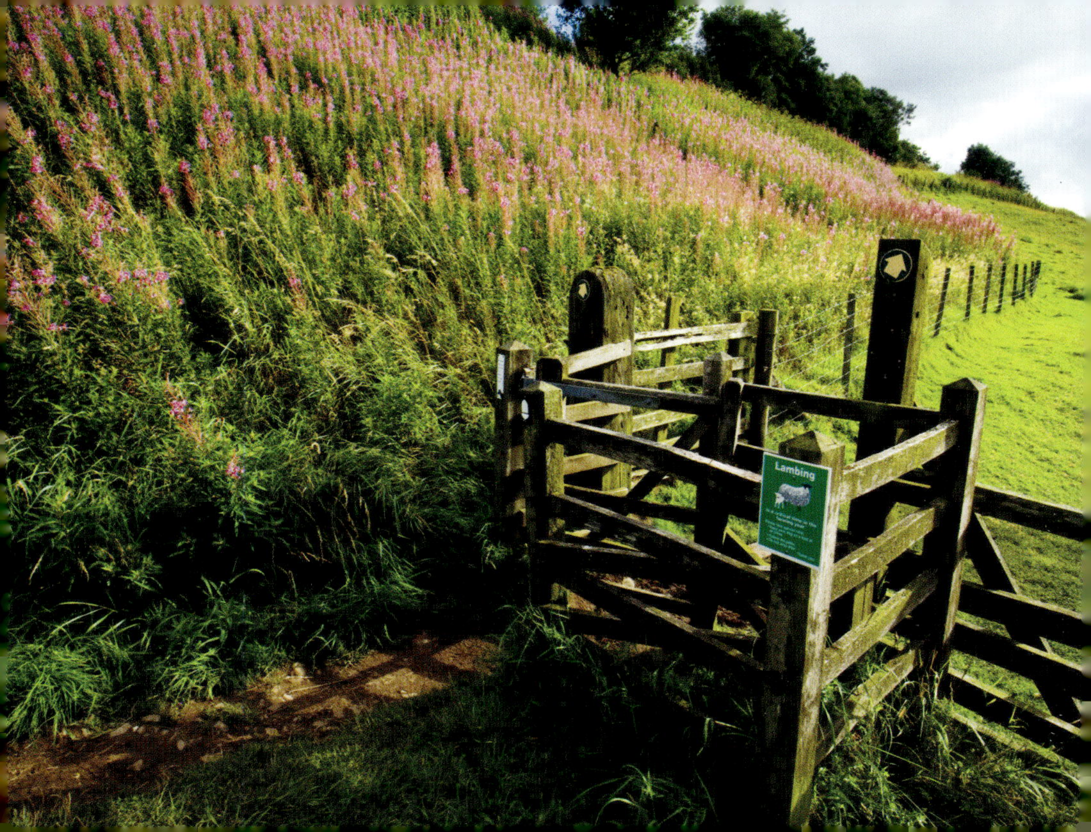
Lambing

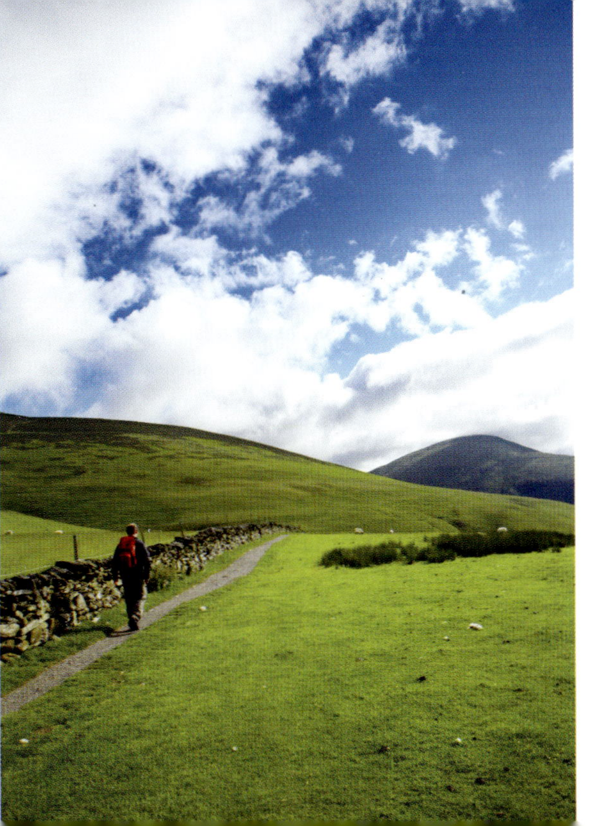

A hiker walking the Cumbria Way long distance route, heading towards Lower Lonscale.

Opposite page:
A glorious display of colour, Rosebay Willow Herb flowering near to a typical stile encountered on the Hadrian's Wall path running through the north east of Cumbria.

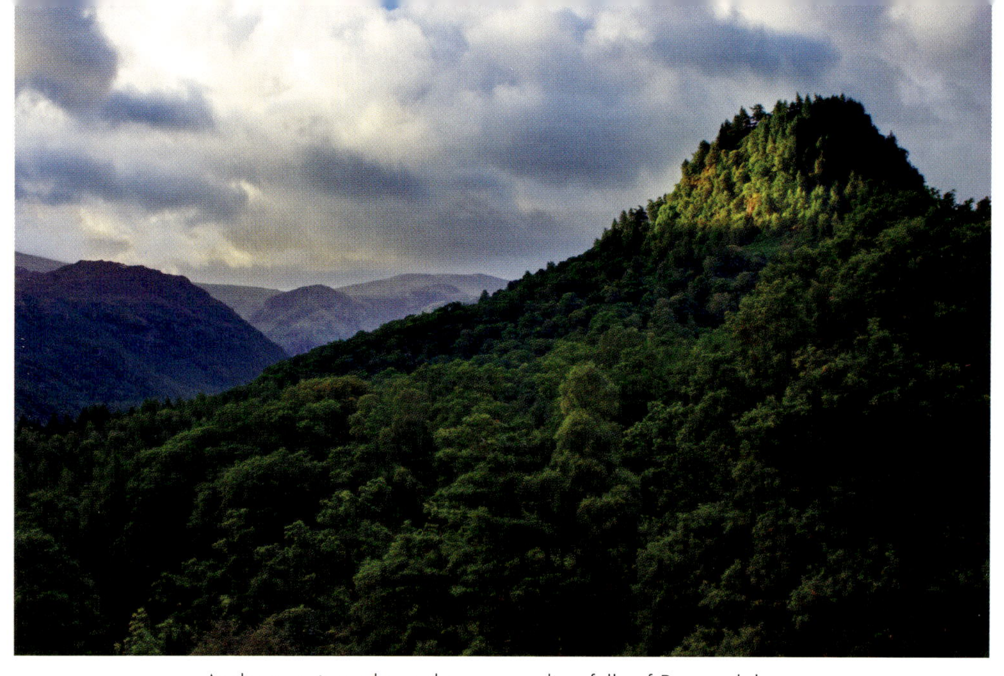

As the sun rises above the surrounding fells of Borrowdale,
it briefly illuminates the densely forested face of Castle Crag.

The late autumn colours of coniferous woodland in Parson's Park near Caldbeck.

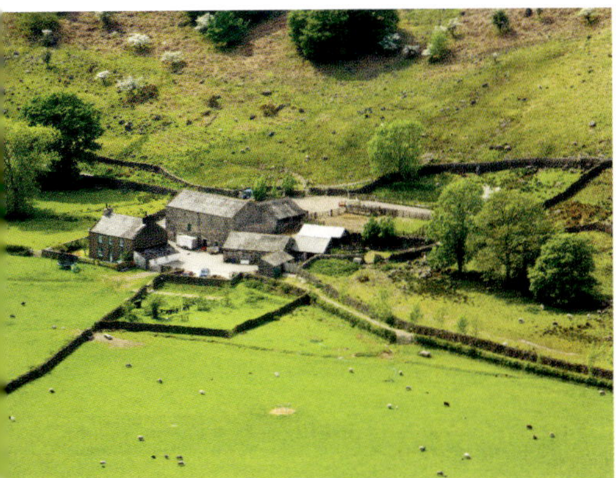

Farm and agricultural land in Eskdale located in the Western Lake District.

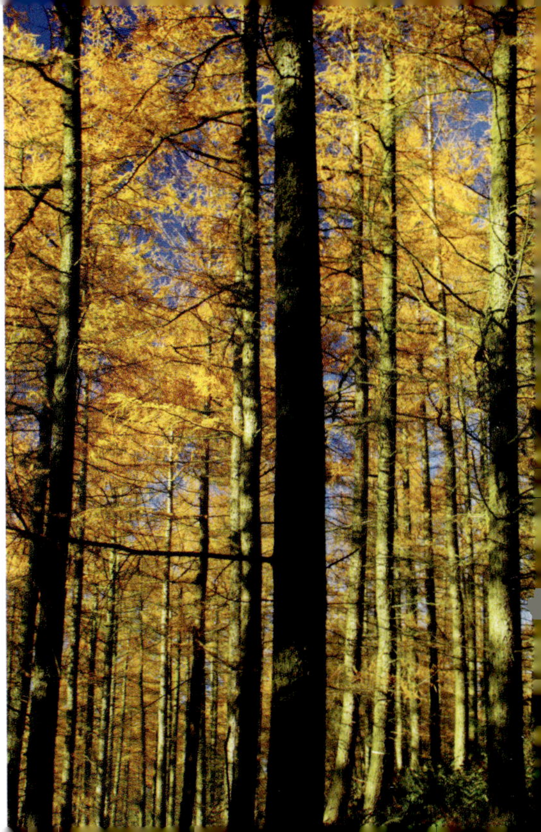

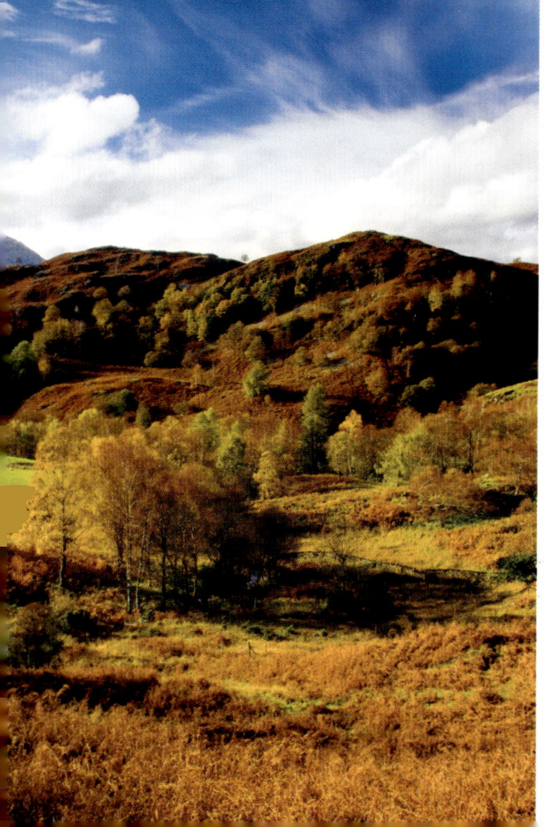

During the autumnal months the vegetation
of Holme Fell transforms the landscape
into a vibrant display of rustic colours.

Opposite page:
A lone tree growing against a traditional
dry stone wall running through Castlerigg
Fell, shortly after a spring snowfall.

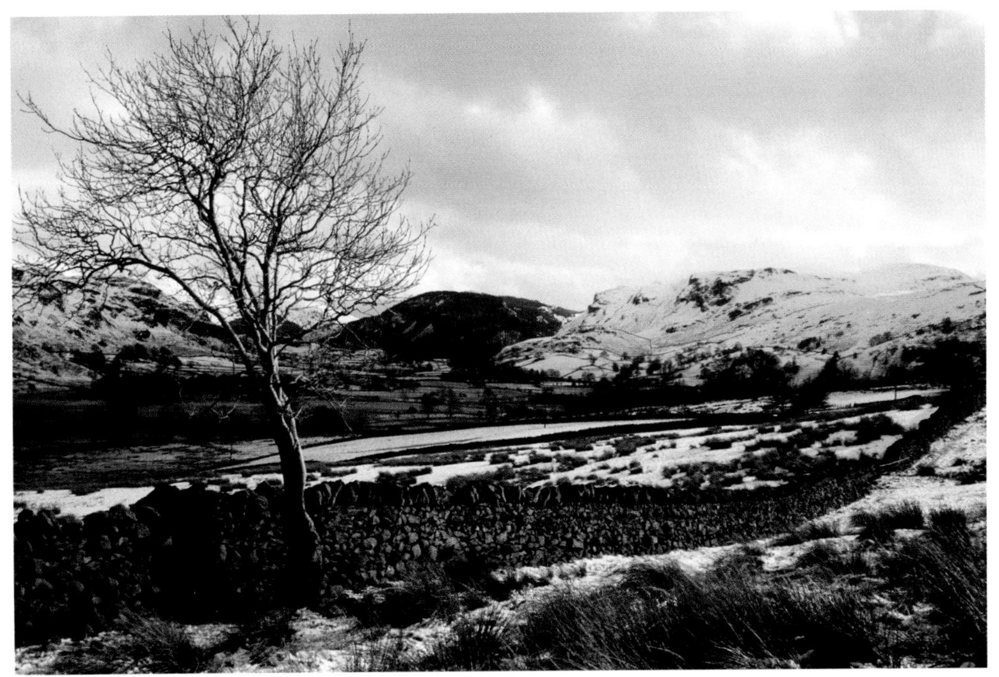

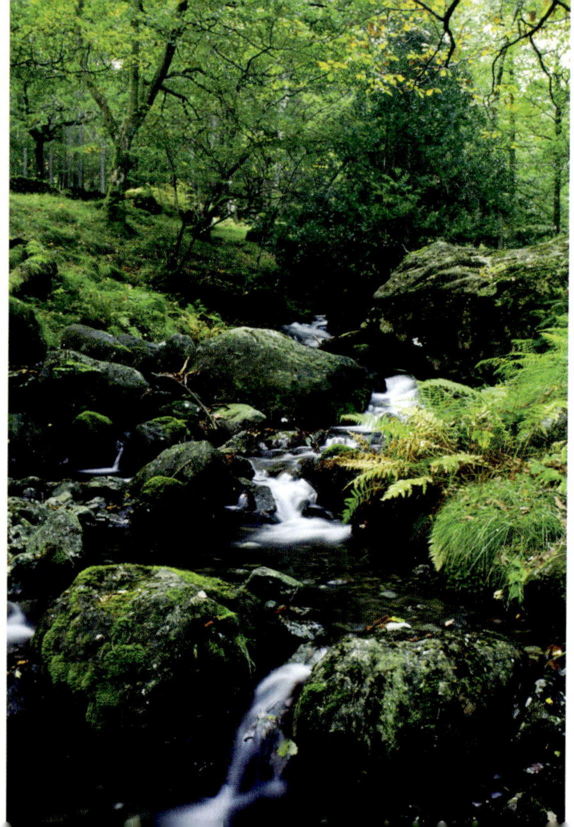

A stream gently meanders through Dalt Wood, National Trust managed woodland near the Grange in Borrowdale.

Opposite page:
Sunset reflected in the mirror-like waters of Wastwater, viewed from the lower slopes of Scafell.

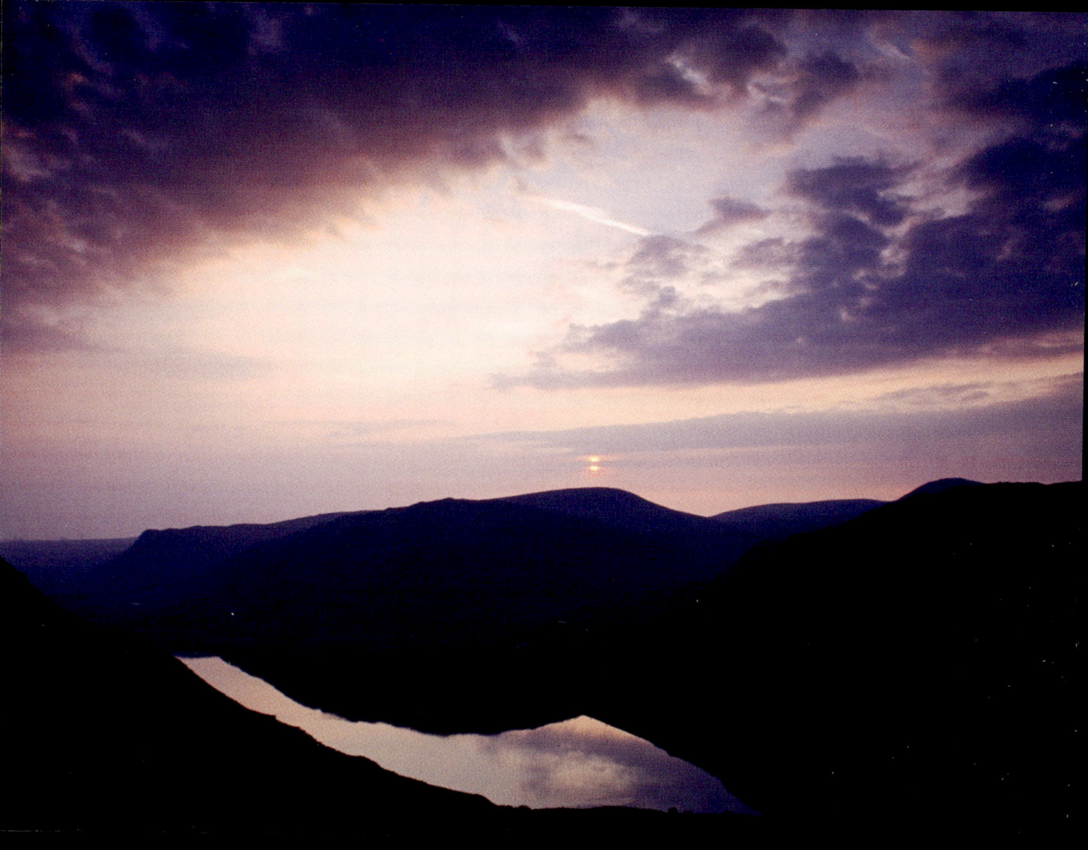

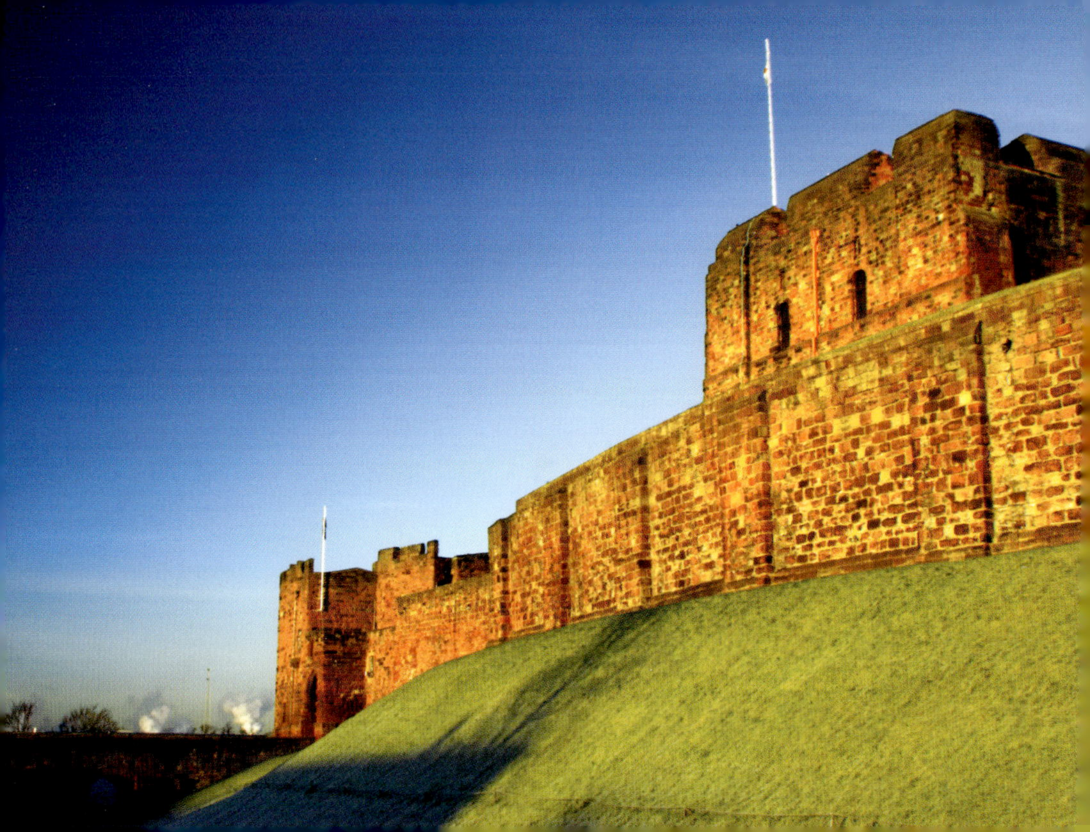

Bell Bridge, spanning
the River Caldrew.

Opposite page:
Early morning winter sun
illuminates the red sandstone
of Carlisle Castle.

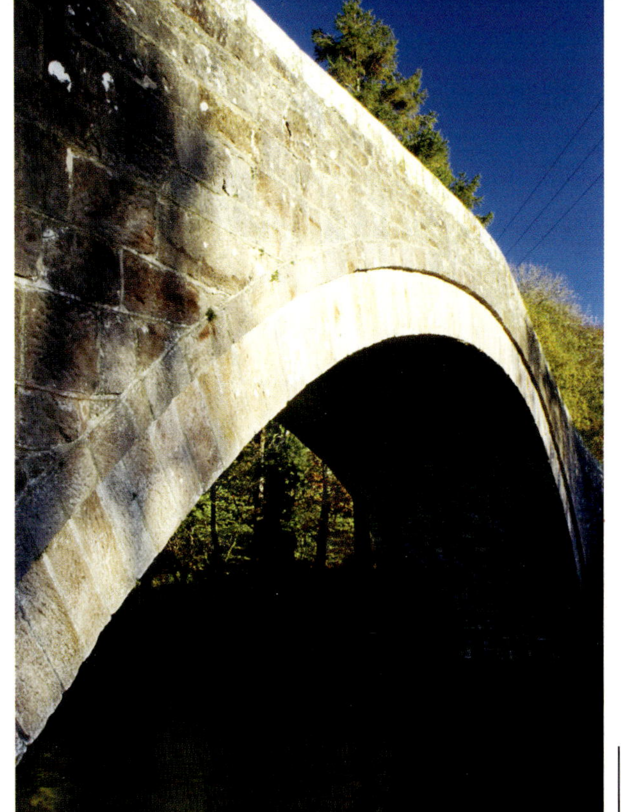

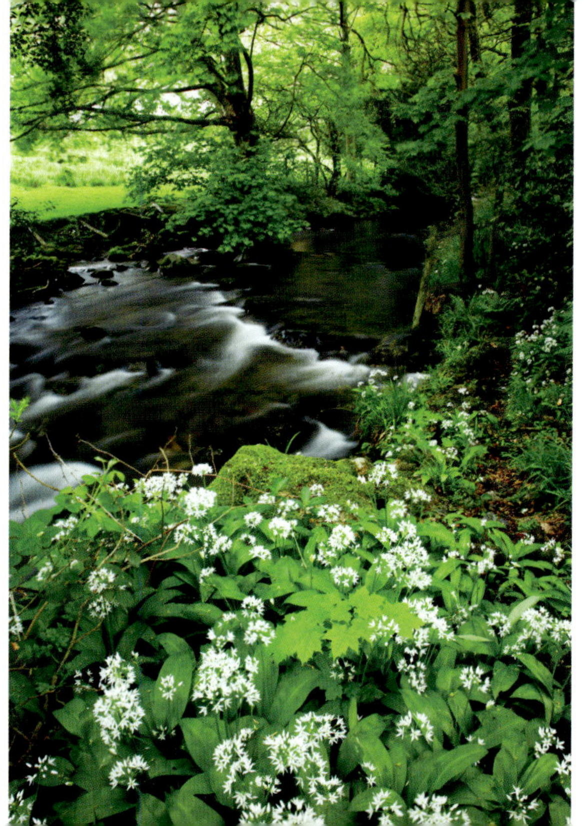

Wild garlic growing
on the woodland adjacent
to Yewdale Beck.

Opposite page:
The rocky lake shore of Ennerdale
Water in the western region of
the Lake District National Park.

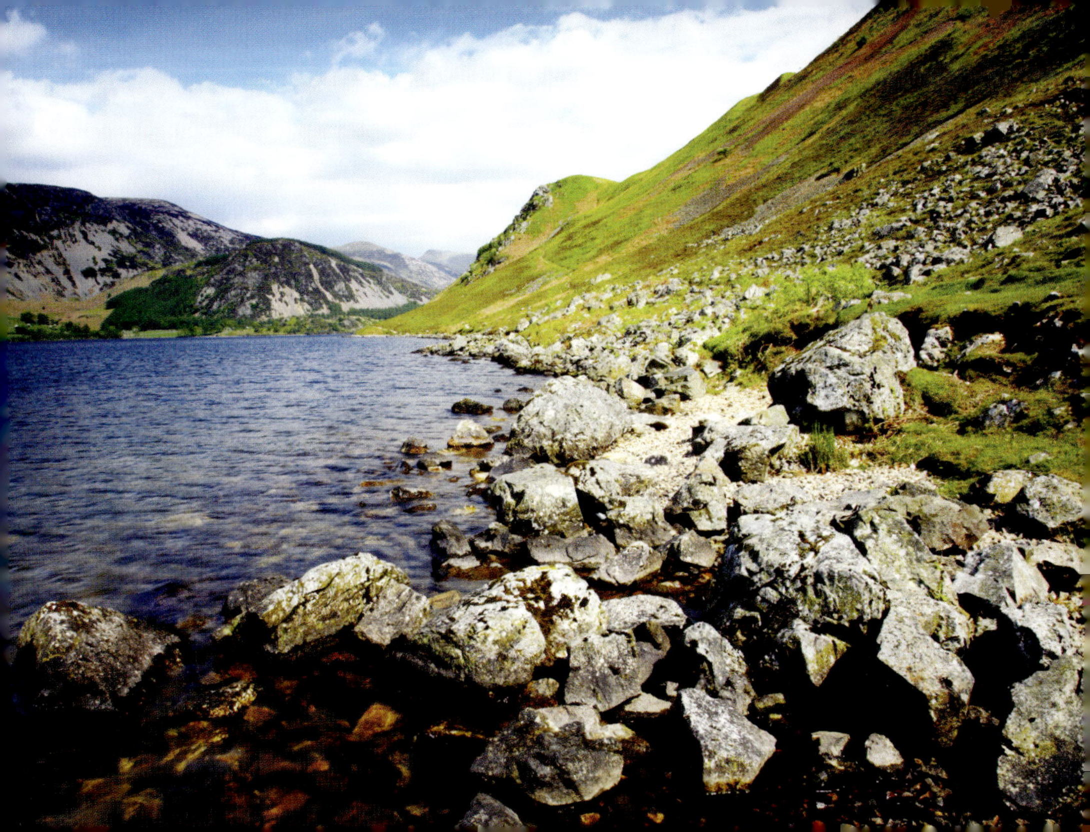

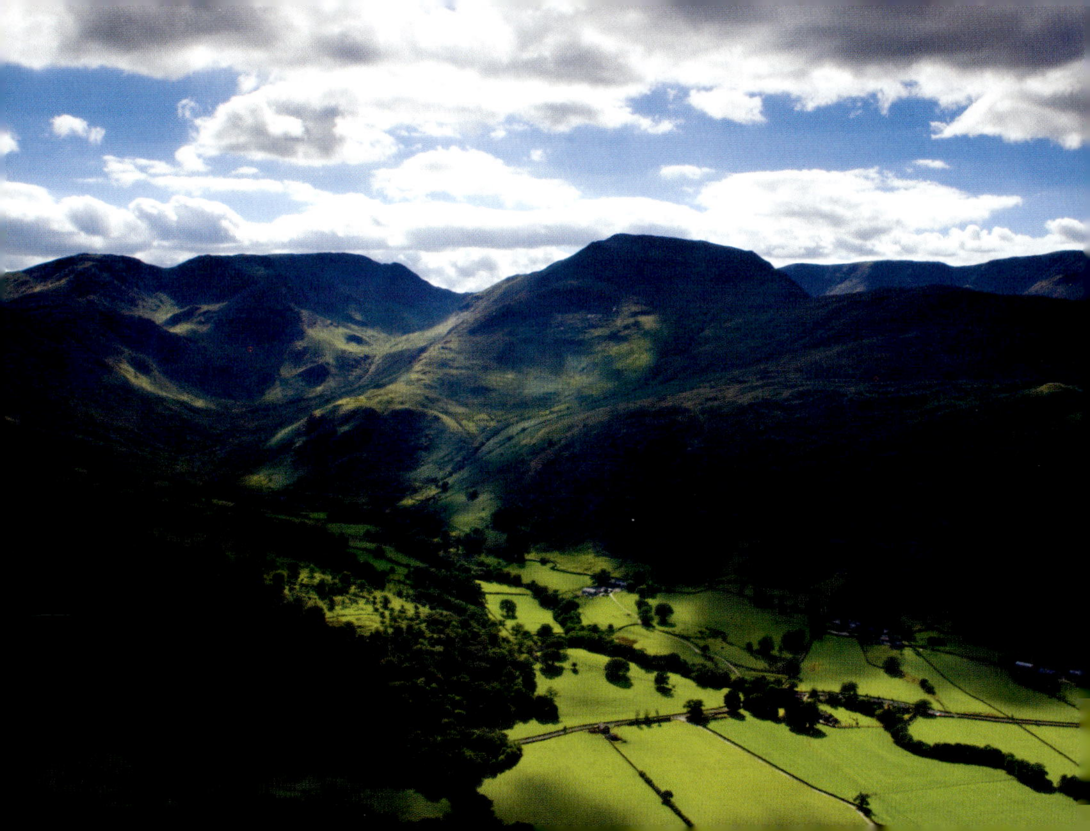

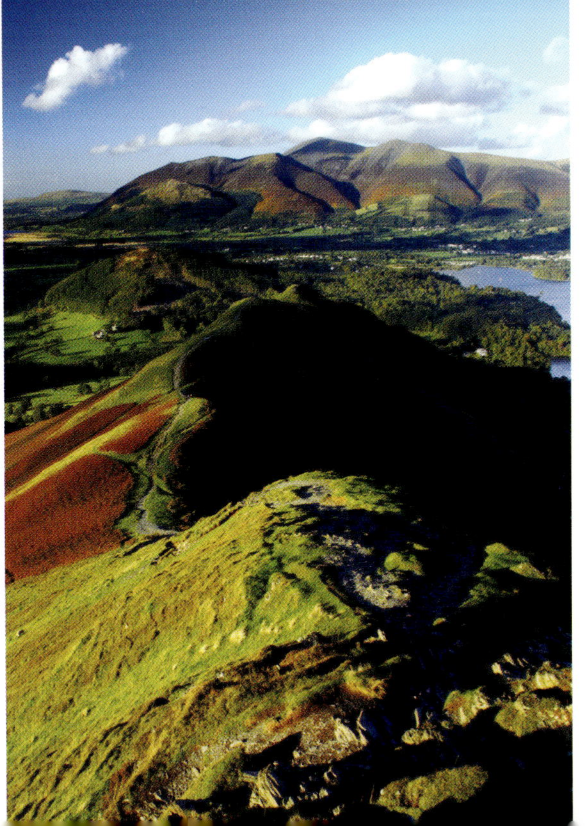

View from Cats Bells near
Derwentwater, looking towards
Skiddaw and Bassenthwaite.

Opposite page:
A clearing storm allows sunlight
to break through onto agricultural
land and surrounding fells of
Grisedale Valley.

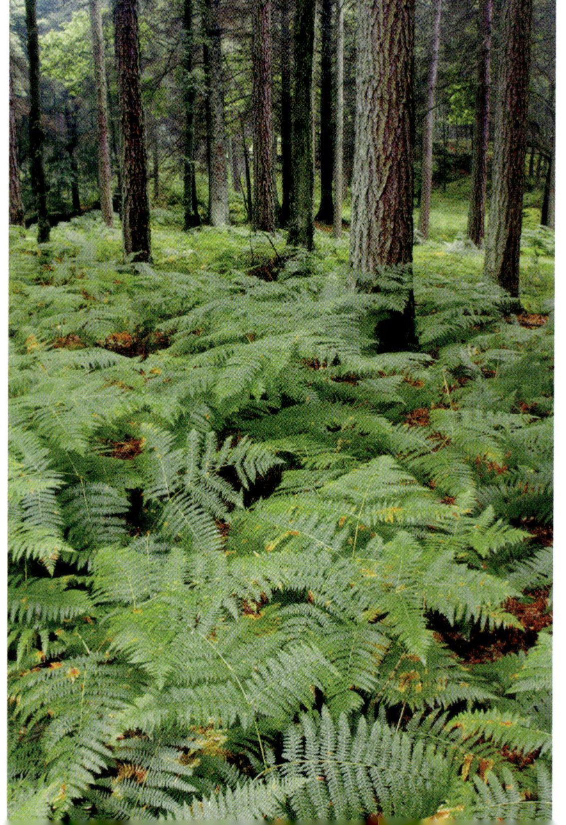

A dense expanse of ferns
growing in Torver Common
Wood beside Coniston Water.

Opposite page:
Ashness Bridge and the fast
flowing rapids of Barrow Beck.

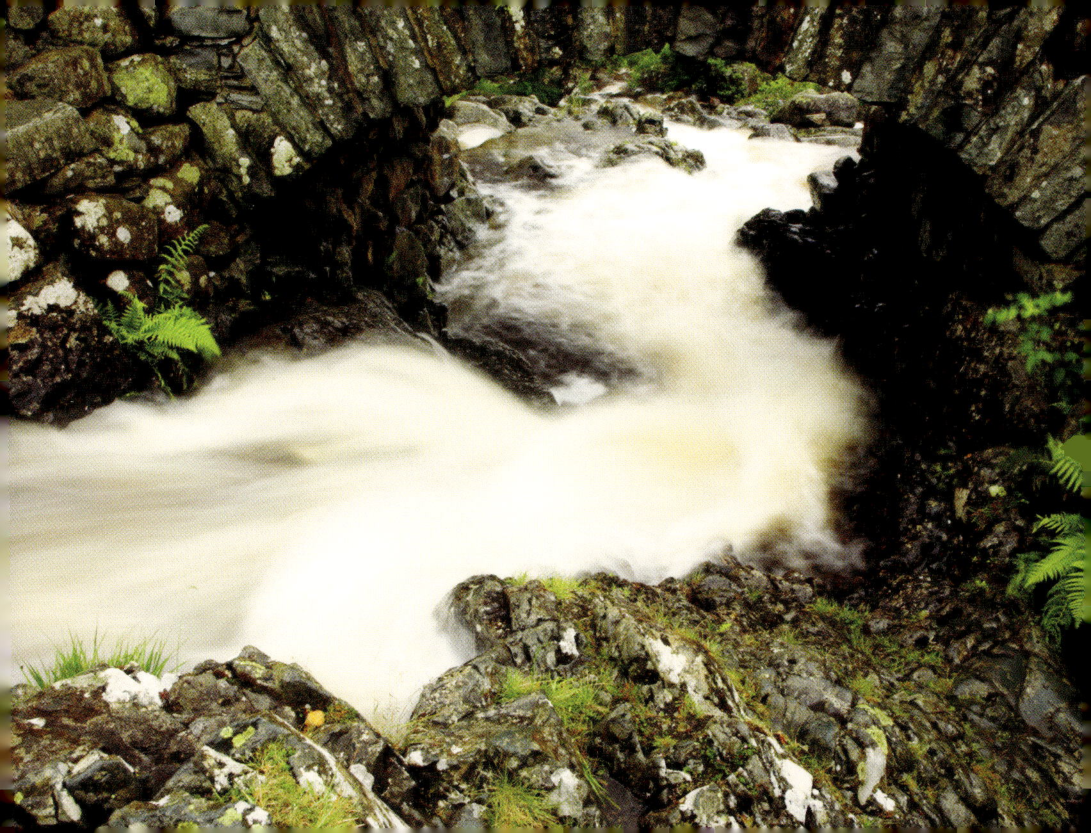

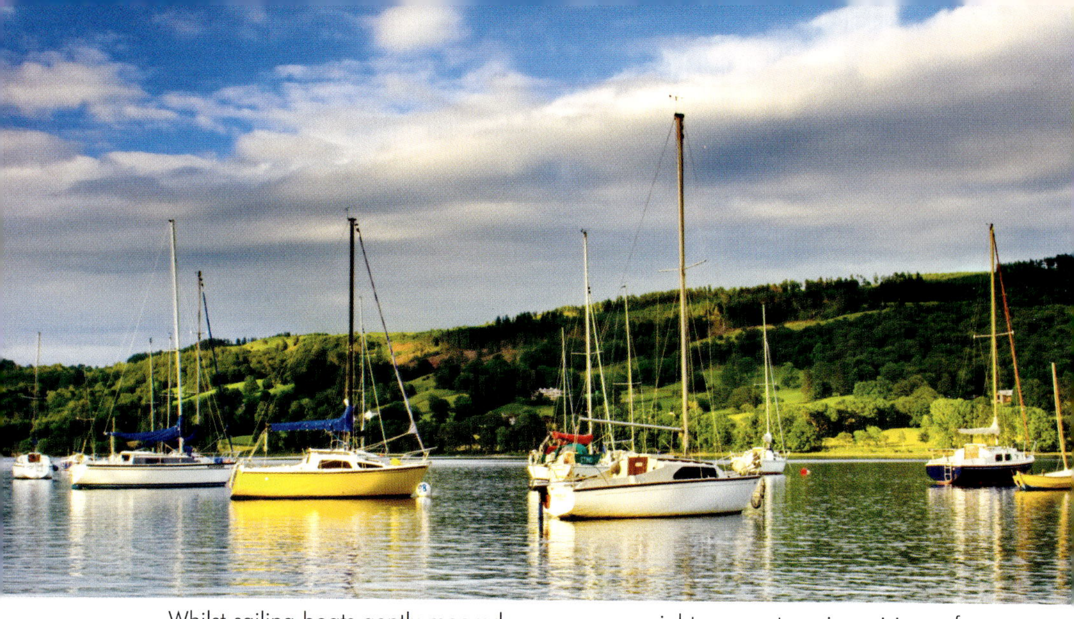

Whilst sailing boats gently moored on a summer night may not conjure visions of record-breaking speedboat attempts, that is exactly what Coniston Water is probably most famous for. Father and son, Sir Malcolm and Donald Campbell, triumphantly made a number of water speed records here during 1939 and 1959. Donald was tragically killed in his jet-powered Bluebird on 4 January 1967.

Birch trees reflected in Tarn Hows, a popular tourist destination once owned by Beatrix Potter. Tarn Hows was actually once two smaller tarns before previous owners merged the two and crafted the surrounding landscape to form the present Tarn Hows.

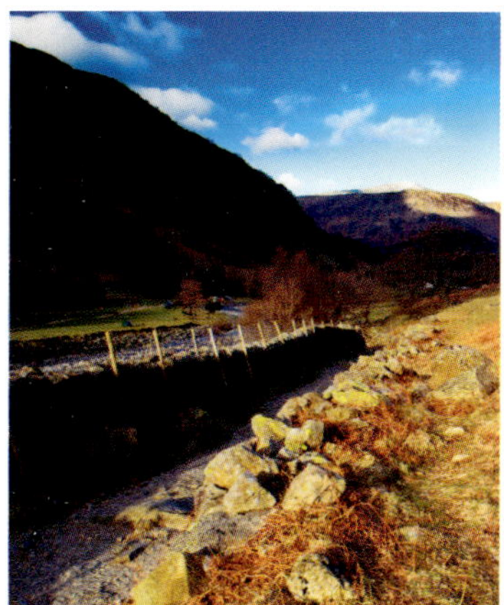

Public footpath near Stonethwaite, heading towards the Borrowdale Valley.

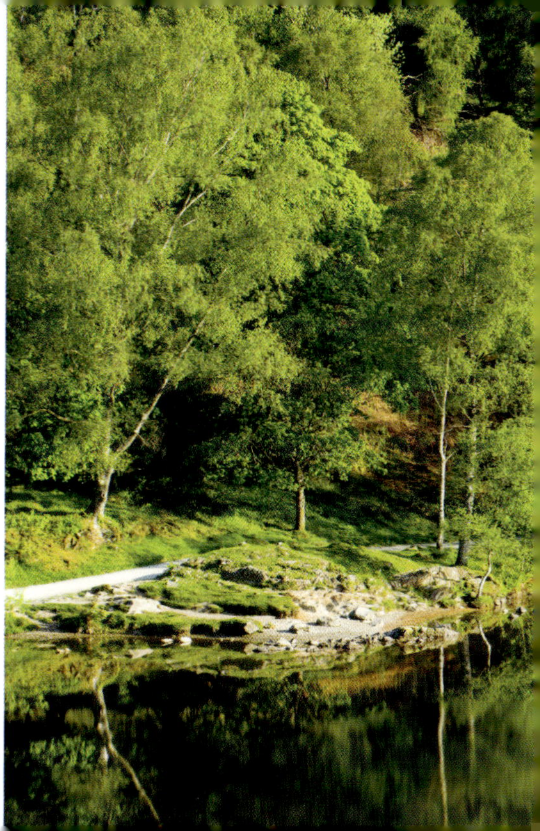

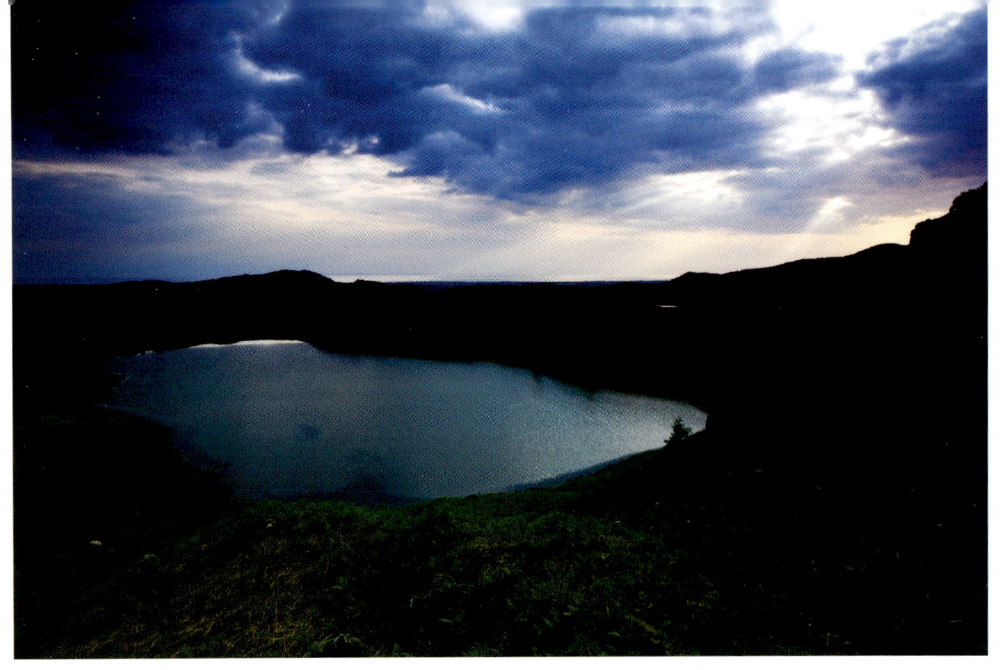

Dramatic clouds over the Irish Sea reflected in Blea Tarn
near Boot in the Western Lake District.

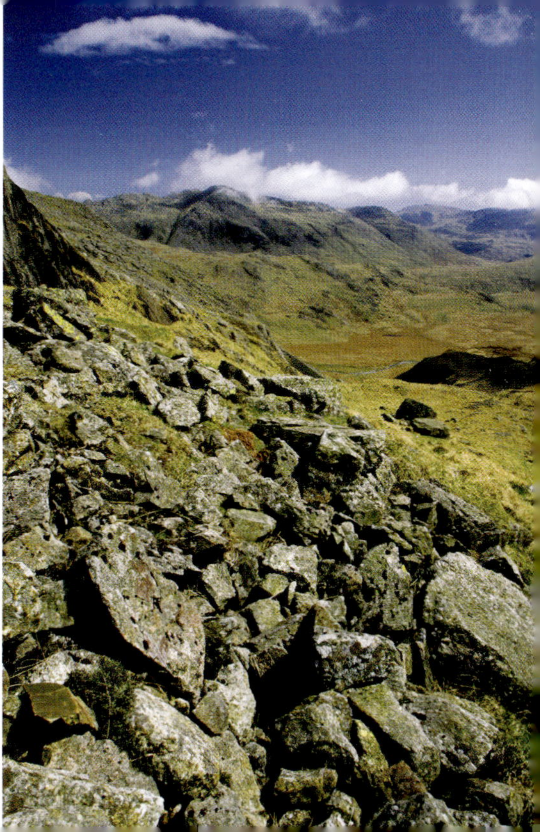

The wild landscape of Upper Eskdale
viewed from below Scafell Pike.

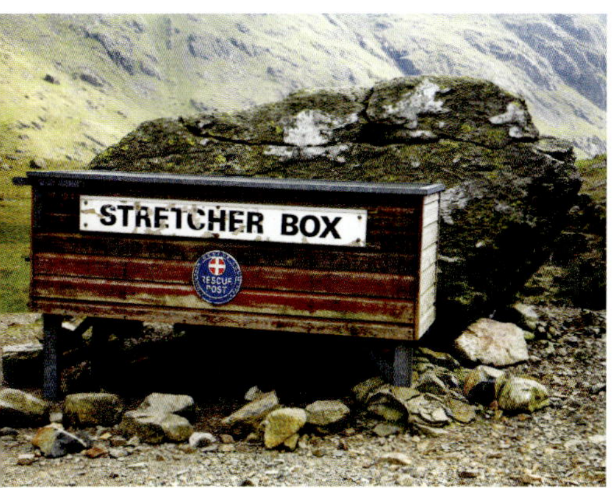

Mountain rescue stretcher box
and rescue post near Great Gable.

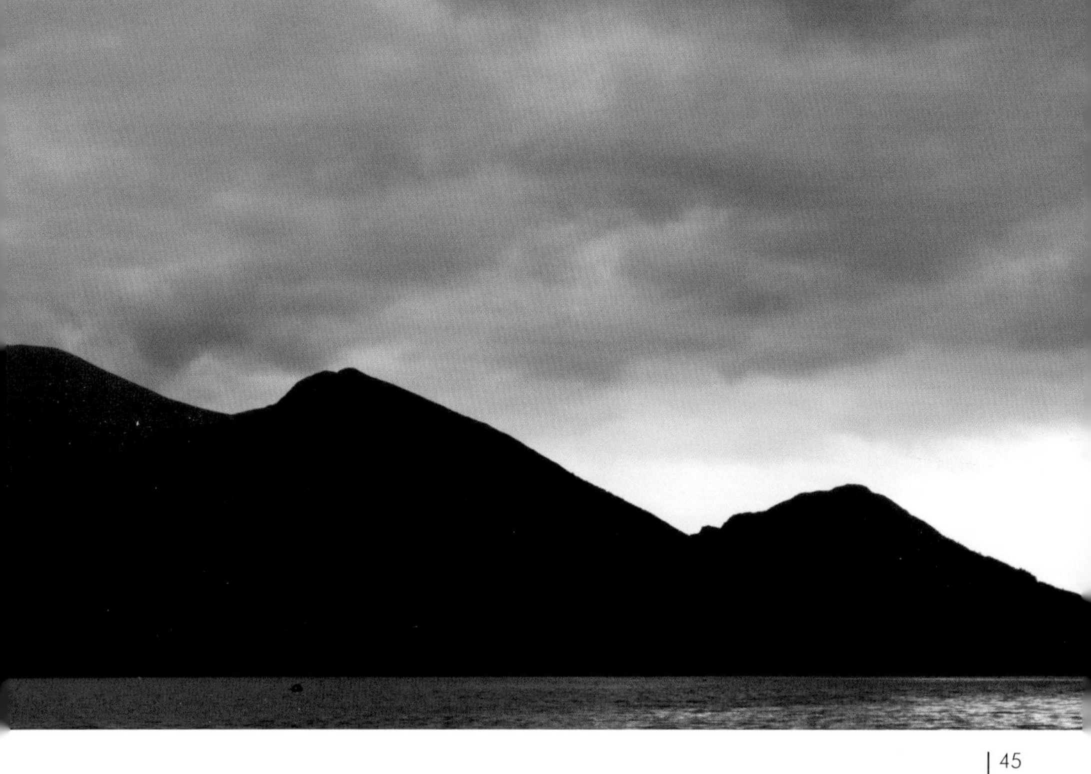

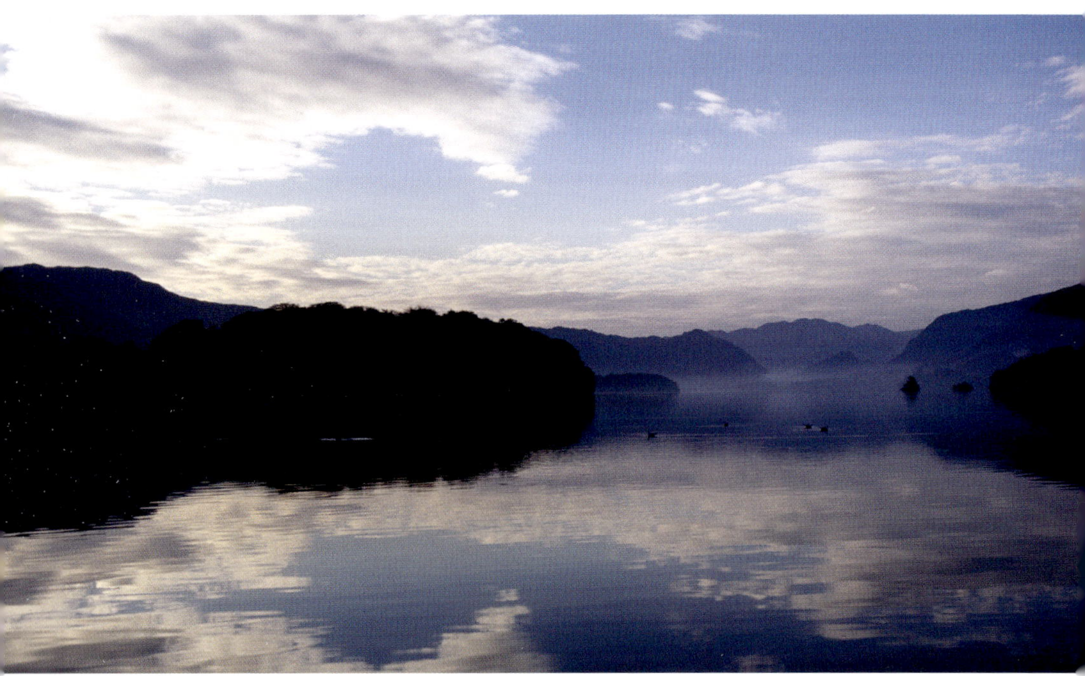

The northern shore of
Derwentwater offers one of the finest
views to be found in the Lake District.
Here an autumn mist rises to reveal the
'Jaws of Borrowdale' and the surrounding fells and peaks, including the
infamous Cats Bells.

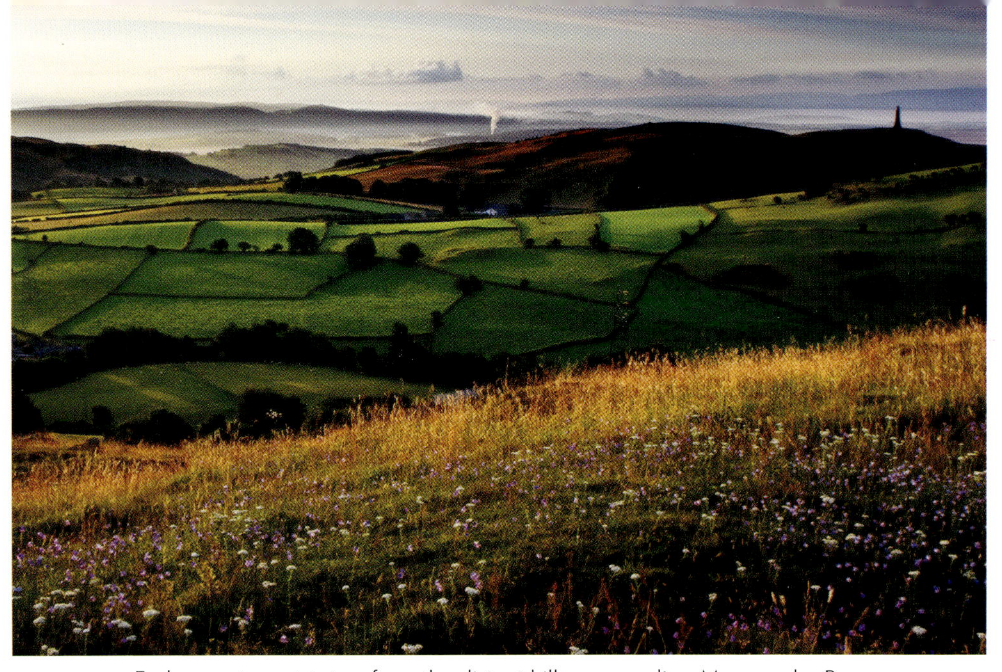

Early morning mist rises from the distant hills surrounding Morecambe Bay,
viewed from farmland above the town of Ulverston.

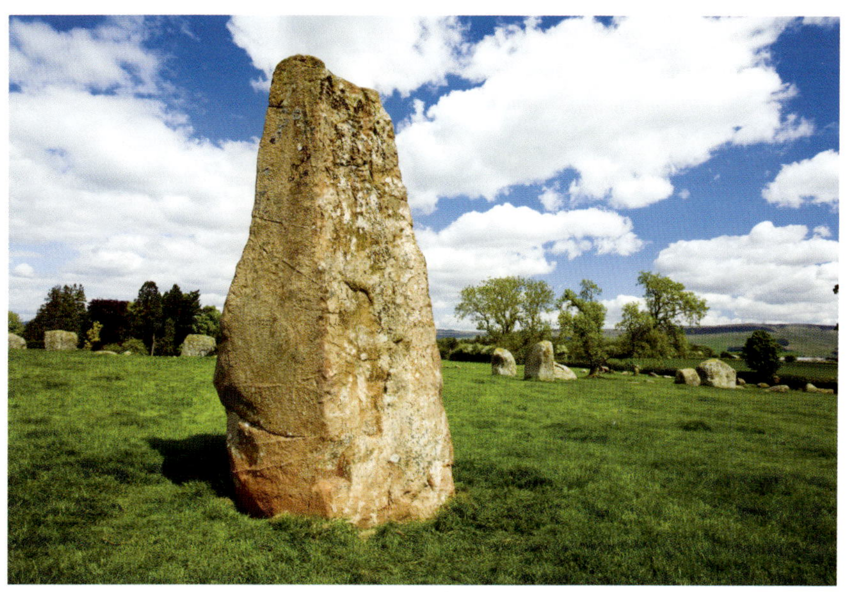

Long Meg and her daughters, one of the finest stone circles
to be found in the north of England.

The Great Langdale Beck running
through woodland near Chapel Stile.

Opposite page:
View from the lower slopes of
Great Gable towards Wastwater
and Wasdale Head.

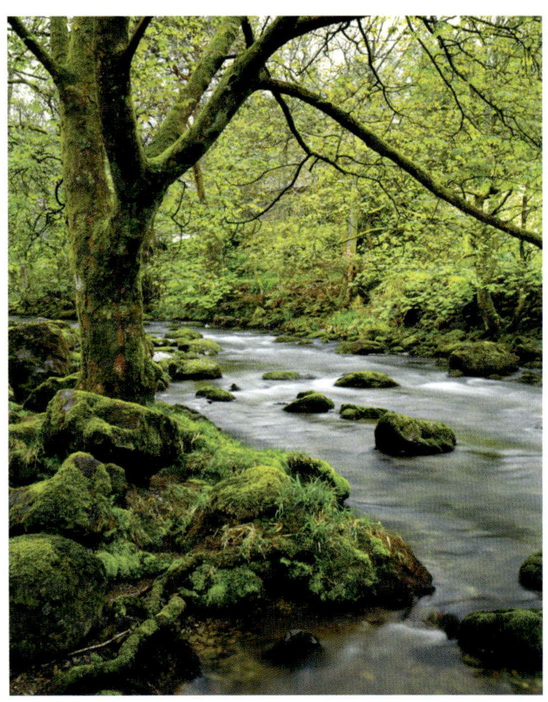

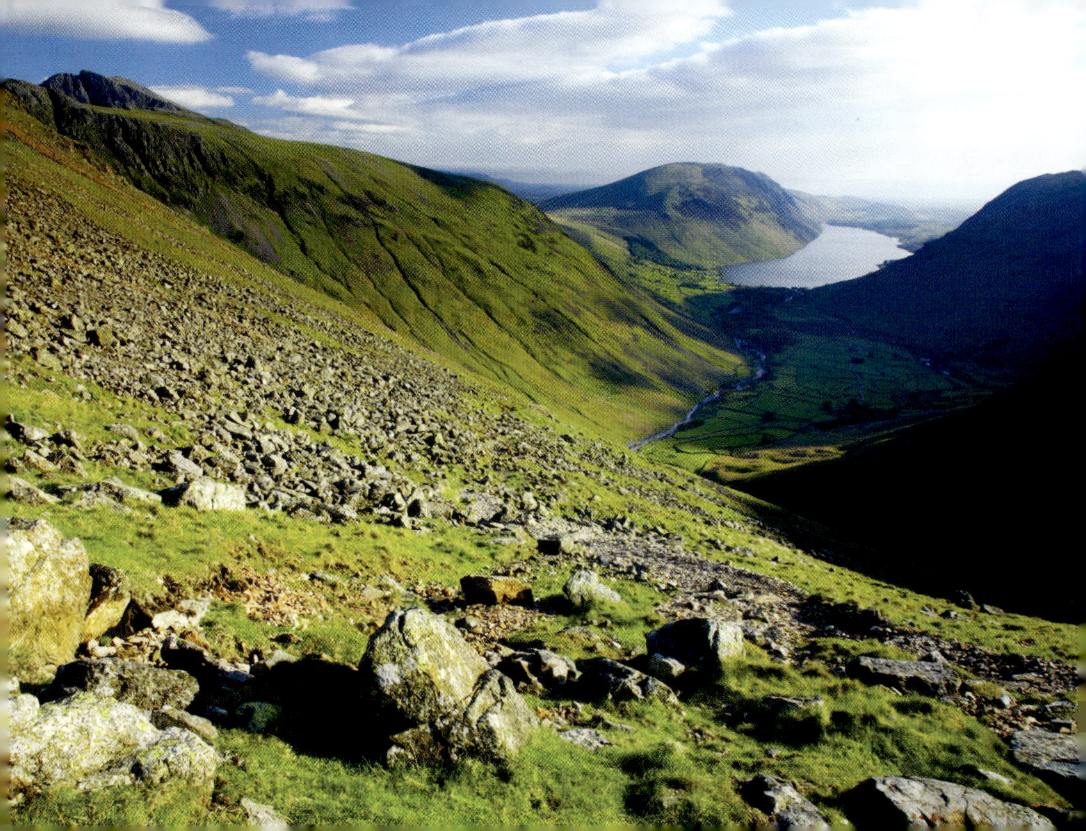

The wild, rocky outcrop of Peathill
Crag near Hardknott Pass.

Opposite page:
Soft light illuminates a
solitary cottage on the banks of
Lake Buttermere, at Peggy's Bridge.

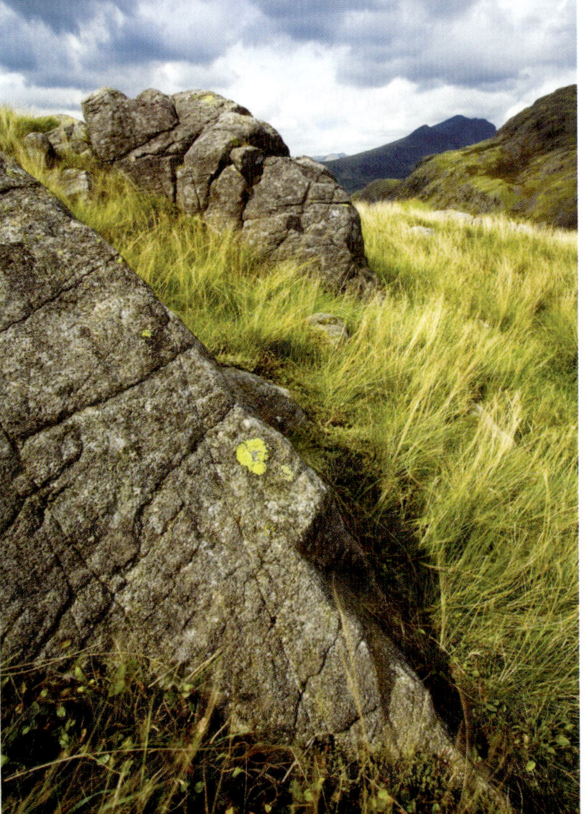

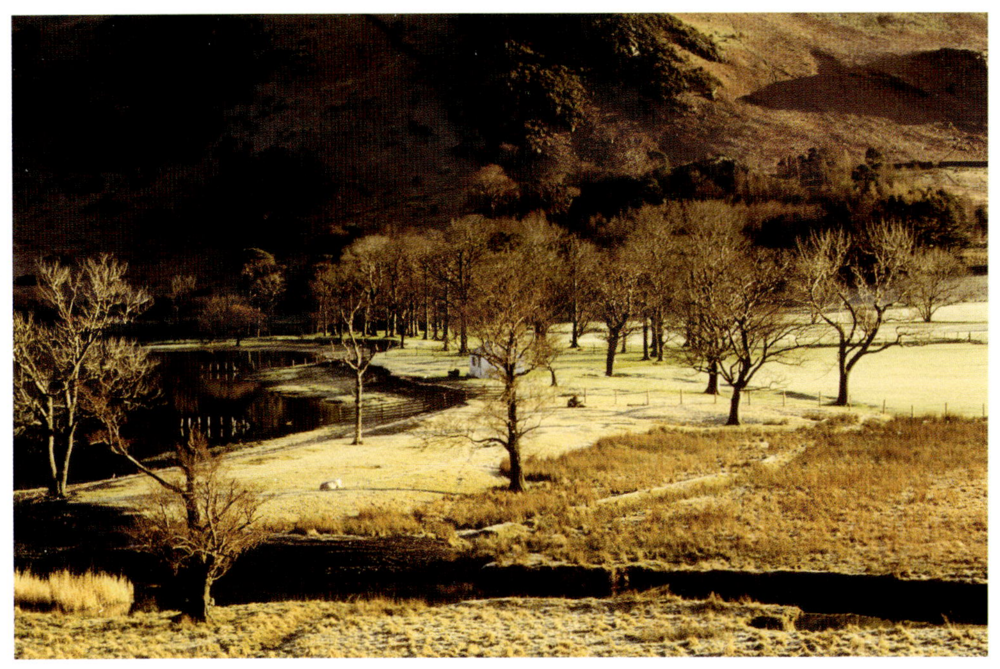

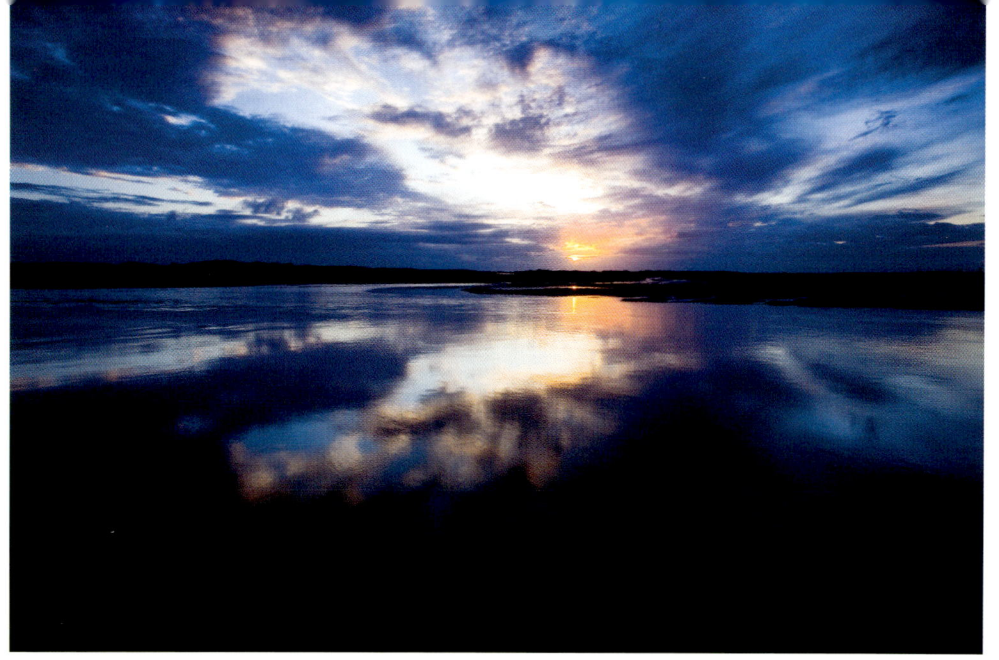

Clearing storm clouds at sunset, reflected in the wide estuary
formed by the merging of the rivers Irt, Esk and Mite.

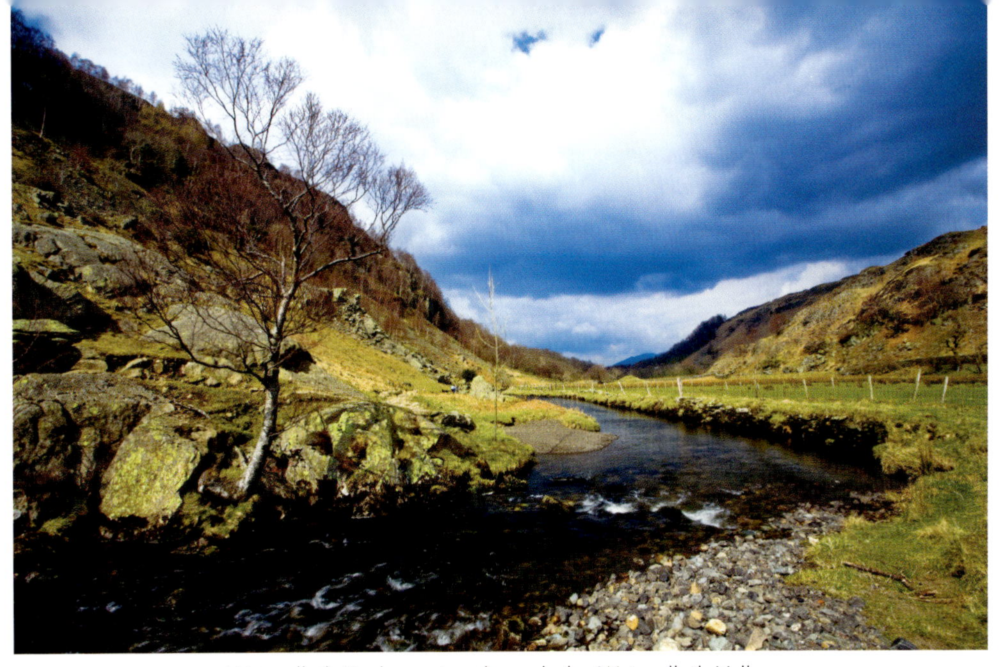

Watendlath Beck running through the Watendlath Valley.

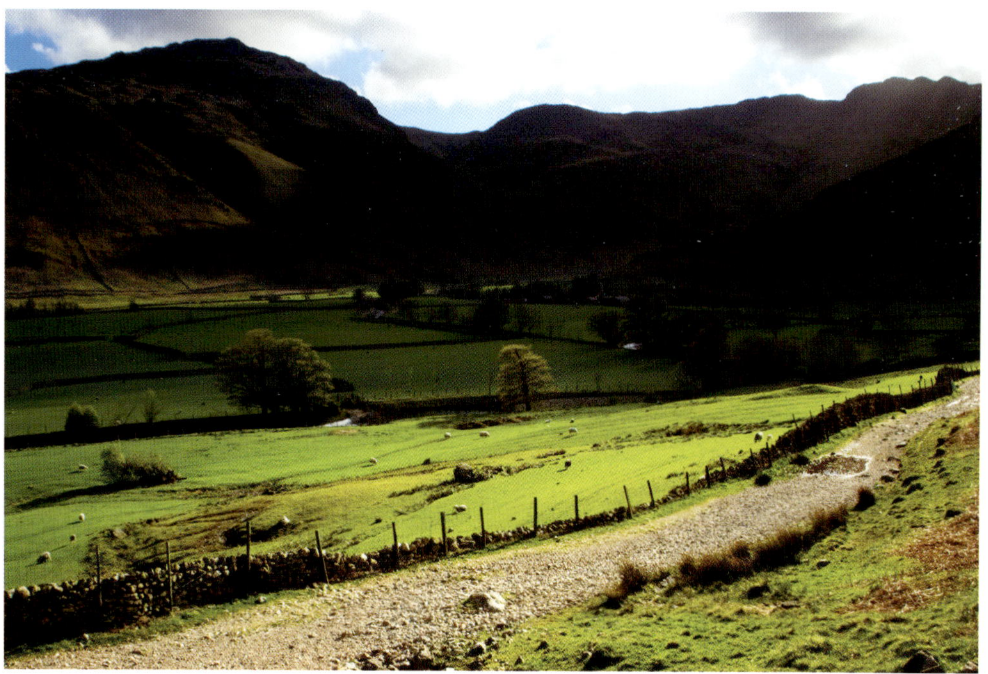

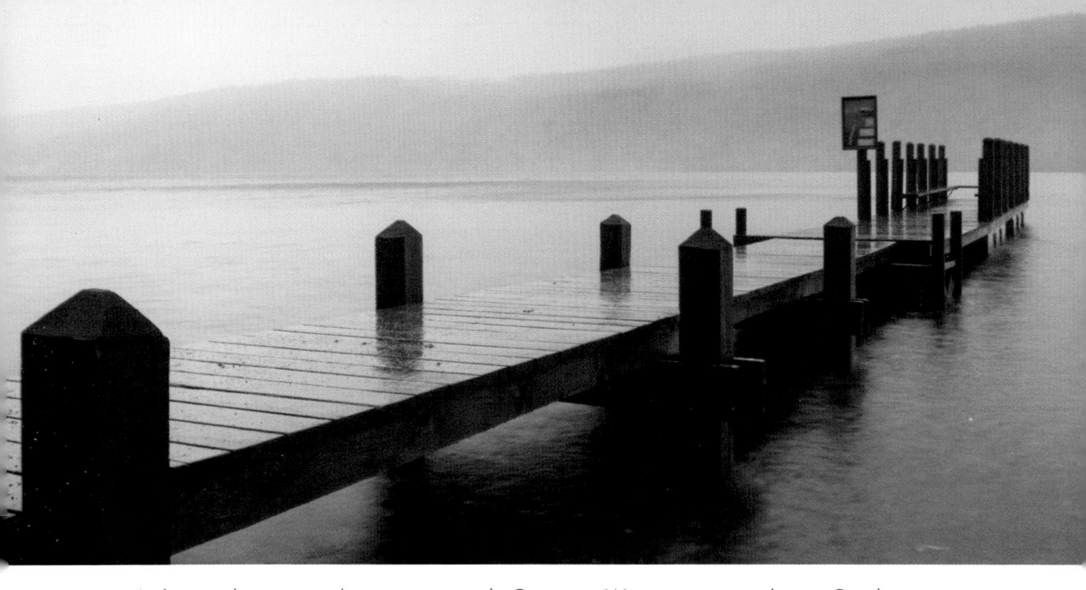

A deserted jetty stretching out towards Coniston Water on a wet day in Cumbria.

Opposite page:
Storm clouds clear above the glaciated valley of Great Langdale at the point where the valley divides at Stool End to form the Mickleden and Oxendale.

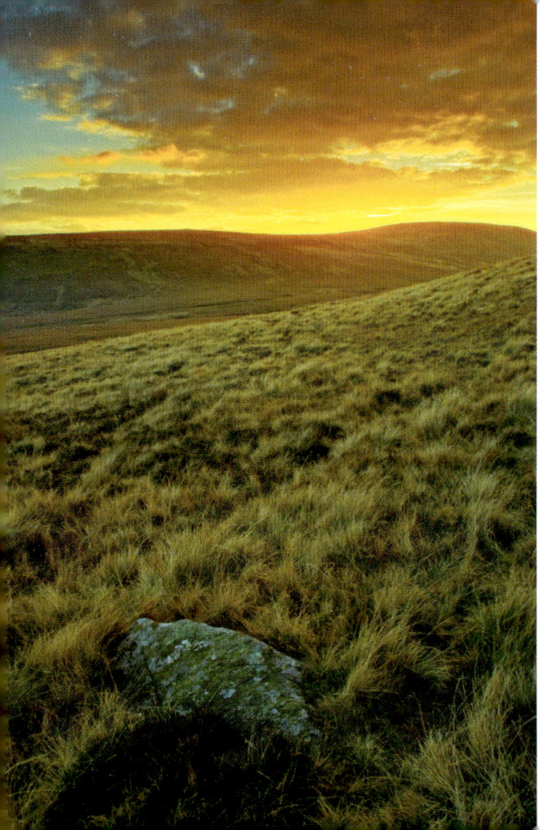

The soft hues of a sunset behind
the tussock-covered hills of the
Caldbeck Fells towards the northern
extremities of the National Park.

Opposite page:
A view towards the distant mountains
of the National Park, looking over the
undulating hills of the distinctive
Howgills massif near Sedbergh.

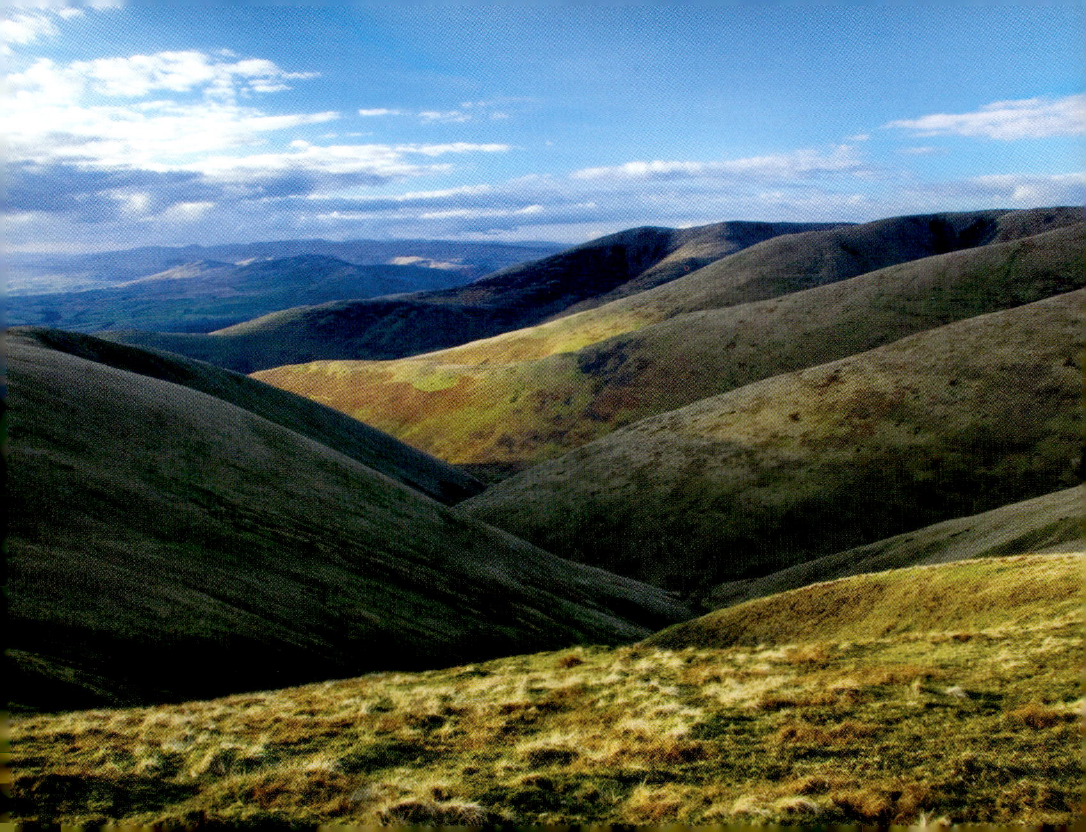

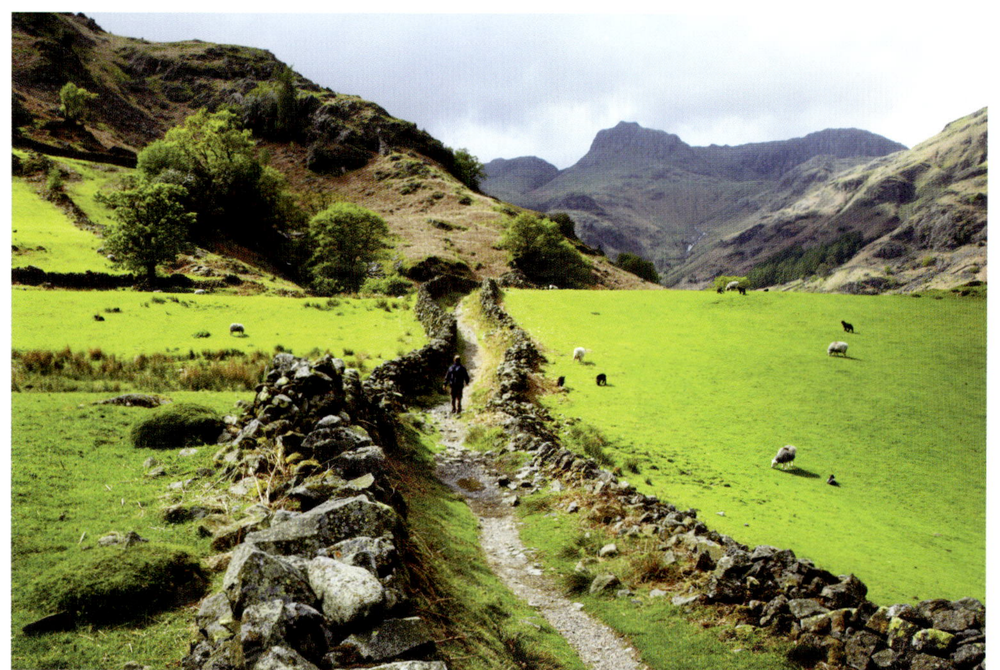

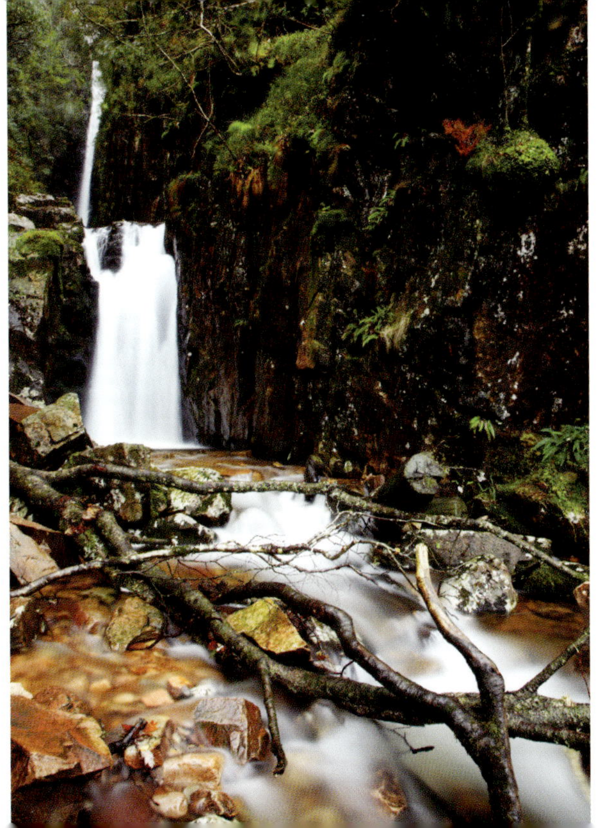

The 170ft drop of Scale Force near the village of Buttermere makes it undoubtedly one of the more dramatic waterfalls to be found within the boundaries of the National Park. The falls have always been popular with tourists and were considered a 'must see' for Victorian visitors on sight-seeing trips to the Lake District.

Opposite page:
A hiker walking along the a public footpath near Chapel Stile, heading towards Dungeon Ghyll and the Langdale Mountains.

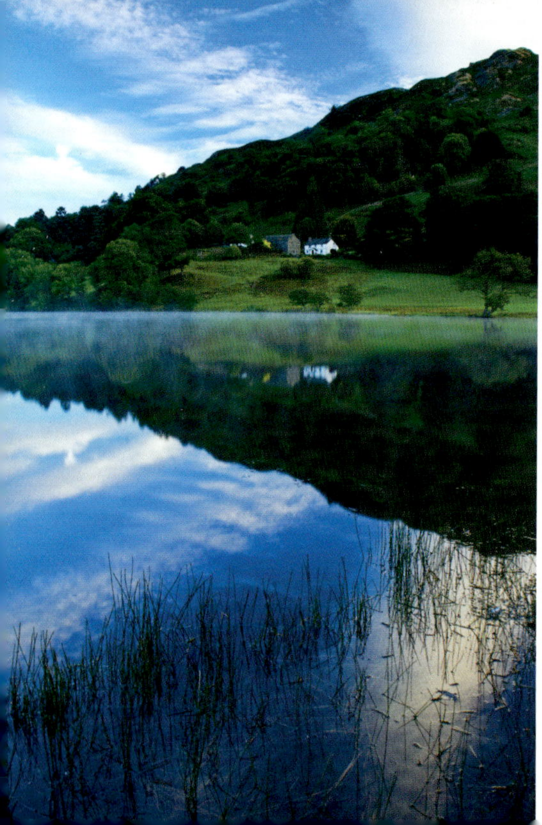

Stereotypical Lake District scenery reflected in the still waters of Loughrigg Tarn.

Opposite page:
The vivid purple of late summer flowering heather growing alongside Glenderaterra Beck.

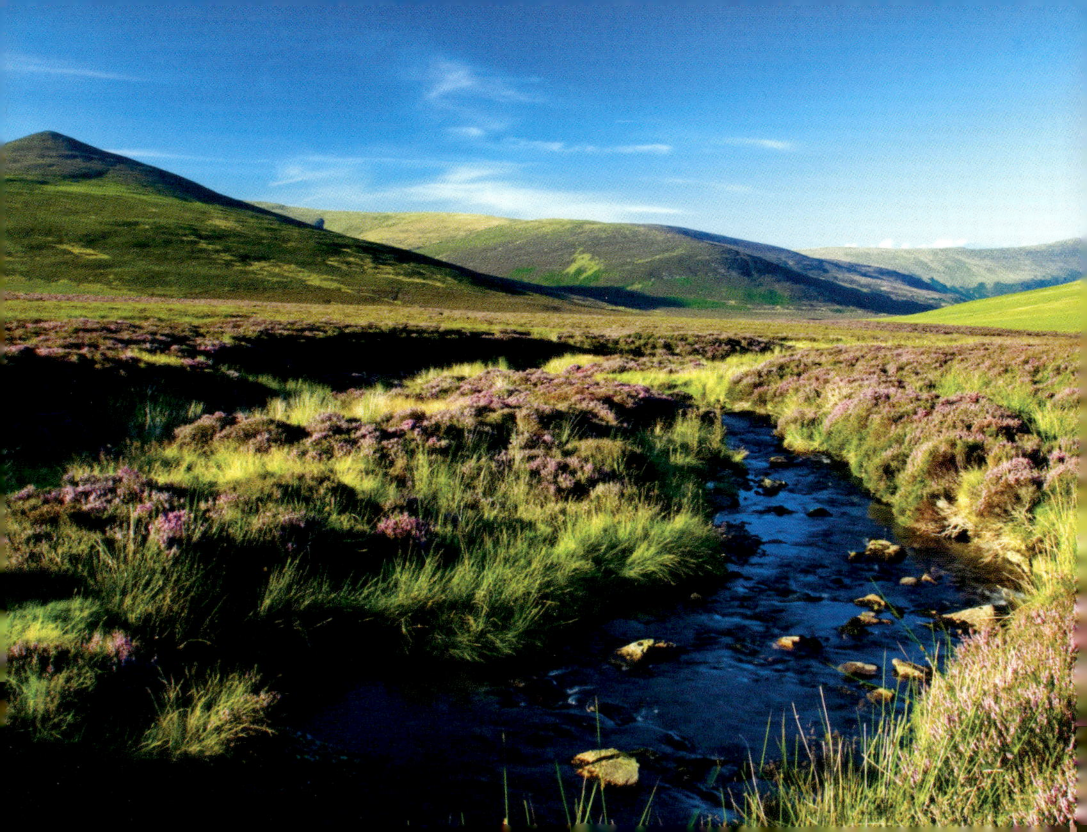

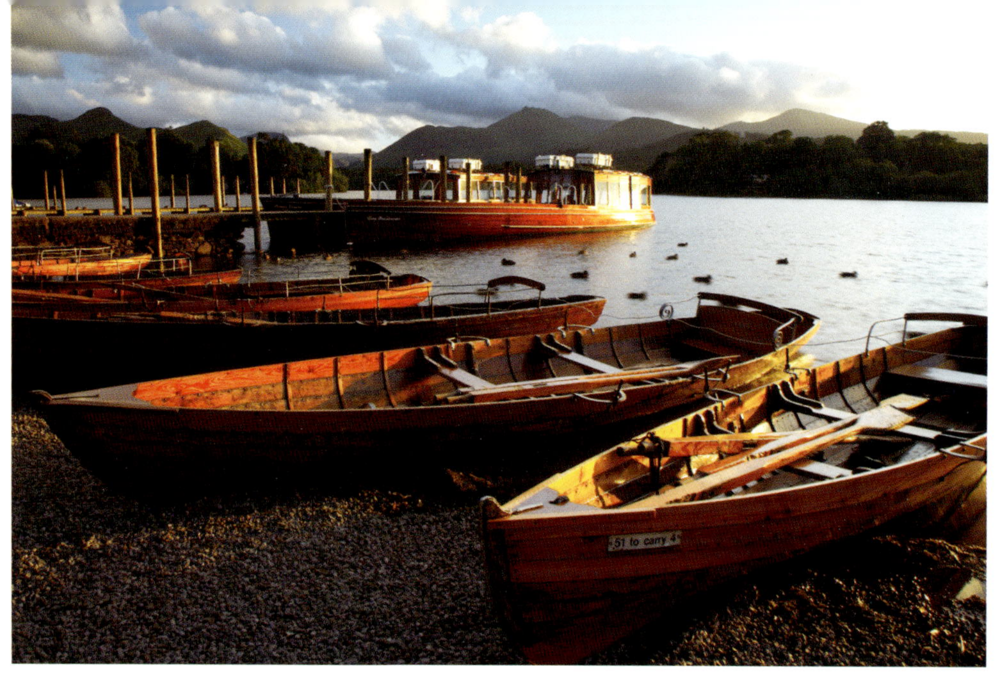

Rowing boats and a tourist cruise ship moored at the popular jetty
on the shore of Derwentwater, near the town of Keswick.